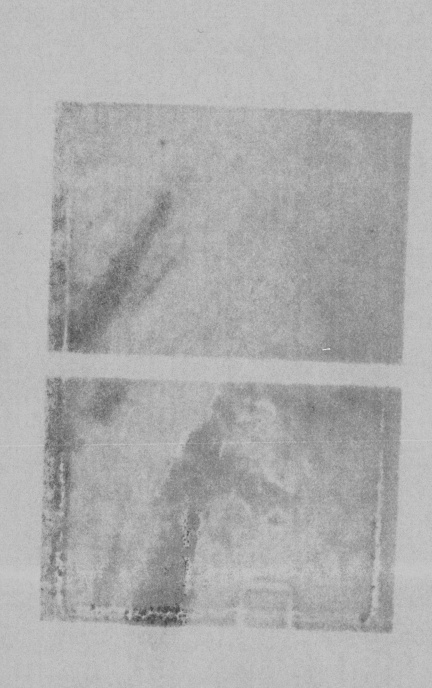

TRANSATLANTIC LINERS
1945-1980

TRANSATLANTIC LINERS 1945-1980

William H. Miller

ARCO PUBLISHING, INC.
New York

to Mother and Dad
who have welcomed me with love at so many piers

Library of Congress Cataloging in Publication Data

Miller, William H., 1948-
    Transatlantic liners, 1945-1980.

    Includes index.
    1. Ocean liners. 2. Steamboat lines. I. Title.
VM381.M45 1981   387.2'432   81-1526
ISBN 0-668-05267-8   AACR2

Published by Arco Publishing, Inc.
219 Park Avenue South, New York, N.Y. 10003

© William H. Miller 1981

Printed in U.S.A.

Contents _____

Acknowledgments

Many hands have assisted with the production of this volume. The author wishes to express his great appreciation to American Export Lines, American President Lines, Frank Andrews, Ernest Arroyo, BCM Pictures, Frank O. Braynard, J. K. Byass, Kenneth F. Key and Canadian Pacific, Carnival Cruise Lines, Michael Cassar, Tomas Cernikovsky, Chandris Lines, Costa Line, Cunard Line, Dominion Far East Line, Donaldson Line, Alex Duncan, Erik Eriksen and the East Asiatic Company Limited, Eastern Steamship Lines, Engler Luftbild, Herbert G. Frank Jr, French Line, German-Atlantic Line, Greek Line, Grimaldi-Siosa Lines, Hamburg-Atlantic Line, Heinz Kalus and Hapag Lloyd Werft, F. W. Hawks, Holland-America Line, Home Lines, Incres Line, Italian Line, Eric Johnson, Michael D. J. Lennon, Julie Ann Low, Mariners Museum, Matson Navigation Company, Vincent Messina, Moran Towing Company, Richard Morse, Nederland Line, New Zealand Shipping Company, North German Lloyd, William C. North, Norwegian America Line, Oranje Line, Orient Overseas Line, Len Wilton and P&O Cruises, P&O-Orient Lines, David Pettit, Polish Ocean Lines, Queen Mary Hyatt Hotel, Real Photographs Limited, B. Reeves, J. F. Rodriguez, Royal Rotterdam Lloyd, Schiffsfotos Hamburg, Roger Scozzafava, Lorre Korechy and Sea-Land Industries Inc., James Sesta, Shaw Savill Line, F. R. Sherlock, South China Morning Post Limited, Miss Ballantyne, Mrs Mitchellhill and Southern Newspapers Limited., Spanish Line, Steamship Historical Society of America, Irene Solleder and Stevens Institute of Technology, Swedish American Line, Todd Shipyards Corporation, United States Coast Guard, Clifford Morgan and United States Lines, United States Navy, R. A. Wardale, World Ship Society Photo Library and Zim Lines.

Introduction

Norwegian America Line's *Stavangerfjord* made the first post-war commercial Atlantic crossing in August 1945, and thereby began the most successful twelve-year period that the Atlantic passenger-ship business has ever known. As quickly as possible, other liners followed, fresh from the shipyards, either having been refitted after strenuous military service or as brand-new replacements. Tens of thousands needed transport: immigrants, displaced persons, diplomats, business executives and developers, the military and, most significant of all, the tourists who signalled the onset of a giant leisure-travel boom.

Some of the pre-war liners returned to service, often with the great popularity and acclaim that they had enjoyed in the Twenties and Thirties. The *Queen Mary* was retained as the impressive flagship of the Cunard fleet while liners like the *Ile de France* and *Nieuw Amsterdam* continued to have devoted followings.

New passenger ships of all types began to appear. American Export's *Constitution* and *Independence* were in the tradition of the classic ocean liners: large, powerful and well equipped. Each could take 1,000 passengers divided into the conventional three classes — first, cabin and tourist. They had spacious lounges, individual restaurants and outdoor lido areas complete with twin swimming pools. Other new vessels had different features. Cunard's *Caronia* could be transferred from North Atlantic to tropical cruise service with absolute ease. Each of her cabins had private facilities, a highly cherished item on the millionaire cruise circuit yet quite uncommon on regular Atlantic ships. Swedish American's *Kungsholm* had all-outside cabins, another novelty, while the superliner *United States* introduced new standards of speed and safety. Holland-America's *Maasdam* and *Ryndam* heralded tourist-class dominance of shipboard accommodation and nicely blended comfort with economy.

The post-war period also saw the introduction of a substantial number of combination passenger-cargo liners. These ships were designed generally as 'assistants' to the larger vessels. They travelled at a leisurely pace, customarily taking more than a week to reach either end, and were appealing owing to their somewhat yacht-like style. The frills of the superliners were missing but there were fine little dining rooms, lounges, and often cabins that were larger (and with private bathrooms, no less) than those found even in first class on the larger flagships. Holland-America's 134-passenger *Westerdam* had its own Palm Verandah while the 'Four Aces' of American Export had permanent outdoor pools for their 125 guests.

The tourist and immigrant ship developed considerably after the war and well into the early Fifties. For example, the Dutch Government took three 'Victory' class freighters and had them rebuilt with 800 one-class capacities; there were fewer cabins and more dormitories. Canadian Pacific operated the *Beaverbrae*, another former freighter, carrying immigrants westbound to Canada and then returning to Europe with freight only. The Swiss-owned Arosa Line had older passenger ships refitted with 'token' first-class sections and large tourist-class areas, the latter frequently being filled to capacity with immigrants and students. These ships responded to the strong demand at the time for inexpensive transatlantic passage. One further development was the appearance of ships of nations as yet virtually unseen on the Atlantic run. Egypt, Yugoslavia, Israel, Turkey and others operated ships or special sailings that met their needs, generally meaning a combination of passengers and cargo.

The business was booming as never before. Profits soared and new liners went on order well into the Fifties. Designers were, however, giving over more space to tourist class with the first-class sections becoming smaller and more exclusive. Holland-America's *Statendam*, which made her debut in 1957, could carry 868 in tourist accompanied by a mere 84 in first class. In the same year, Cunard's *Sylvania* appeared with 154 first class and 724 tourist class.

In October 1958, a jet airliner flew the Atlantic for the first time and the entire pattern suddenly changed. It seemed shocking. Board-room members of some of the great steamship firms strangely saw air travel as a 'fad', and were convinced that tourists, or at least a good percentage of them, would prefer ocean-liner crossings. Sadly, it was a large miscalculation. By 1959, the airlines had secured 63 per cent of all Atlantic passenger traffic: 1,539,934 by air against 881,894 by sea. The trend intensified steadily.

The liners fast began to leave service. The older ships went first, then the combo-vessels all but disappeared. The dormitory-style tourist ships went as well. By 1965, ships like the Cunard *Queens* and the *United States* were deficit-ridden (as much as £750,000 each for the *Queens* two years later). Steamship lines searched for new employment for their ships; Cunard's once highly popular *Mauretania* was painted in 'cruising green' and sent off to the Mediterranean for crossings to New York, then on long cruises and finally given out to charter. Nothing seemed to work. She — like many others — was sent prematurely to the shipbreakers.

Entire passenger lines disappeared, some to concentrate on freight services and others into liquidation. Some of the few liners which endured the initial aircraft crunch were victims finally of the fuel crisis of the early Seventies. Passenger ships were bigger burdens than ever to their owners and a liner like the eighteen-year-old 20,000-ton *Southern Cross* was sold off for a fractional £500,000 in 1973.

Currently the North Atlantic passenger lanes are all but empty, with just a few liners surviving. Most of the ships included in this book have gone to the scrapyards while some, more fortunate, have found new careers in cruising. In all, these passenger liners are the only survivors of the last great transatlantic fleet.

William H. Miller
Jersey City, New Jersey

Steamship Lines

American Banner Lines was a short-lived firm aimed at capturing the peak tourist trade of the late Fifties. Its creator, Mr Arnold Bernstein, had been interested in pre-World War II Atlantic passenger shipping with the Bernstein Line of Hamburg. American Banner lasted a mere fifteen months.

American Export Lines began as a freighter company just after World War I and turned to passenger ships in 1931. The line merged with the American-flag Isbrandtsen Company in the early Sixties and was thereafter known as American Export-Isbrandtsen Lines. Passenger services ceased in 1968, a victim of rising operational costs.

American President Lines came into being in 1938 as a successor to the original Dollar Steamship Lines. Atlantic passenger service was reduced to 12-passenger freighters by 1965 and then discontinued completely. Currently, American President is a Pacific and Indian Ocean container-cargo firm.

Arosa Line was Swiss-owned with Panamanian registry and was founded in 1952 for the purpose of transporting immigrants and low-fare tourists. It was a victim of over-extension and was forced into bankruptcy in late 1958.

Baltic Steamship Company was created after World War II as the Baltic Sea, Leningrad-based, division of Sovtorgflot, the Soviet Ministry of Shipping. It exists at present as the operator of a large passenger and cargo-ship fleet.

Canadian Pacific Steamships Canadian Pacific opened its trans-Canadian railway system in 1887, a Pacific passenger service in 1889 and finally a transatlantic liner run in 1903. The latter operation survived until 1971, when it was forced out of business by declining trade requirements.

Chandris Lines had cargo-ship interests well before, but did not establish passenger-ship services until 1959. At first it was involved in the Australian immigrant trade and then occasional Atlantic crossings began in the Sixties. The final New York to Southampton sailing occured in 1973; the present schedules are completely geared to cruising.

Cogedar Line was developed in the mid-Fifties for immigrant runs to Australia and later offered student voyages on the North Atlantic. It was absorbed by the Costa Line in 1968 and completely lost its identity.

Companhia Colonial discontinued its Atlantic passenger service in 1973 and later ended its African passenger runs as well. The company's freighter runs continue at present.

Costa Line has grown to become the world's largest passenger-ship operator (as of 1980), apart from the Soviet Union's Merchant Marine. Costa was created in 1948 for the South American immigrant trade.

Cunard Line is probably the best-known transatlantic steamship company name. It was founded in 1838 and the first service to Boston started two years later. In 1934 it merged with the White Star Line and, until 1950, was known as Cunard-White Star Line.

Donaldson Line was first organized in 1855 yet it did not establish a service to Canada until 1876. The passenger run was ended in 1966 and shortly thereafter the entire fleet was disbanded.

Dutch World Services was a composite name in the Fifties and early Sixties for the periodic sailings of passenger ships of the Nederland Line and Royal Rotterdam Lloyd on the North Atlantic run.

East Asiatic Company is one of Denmark's foremost steamship companies; it started Atlantic services in 1946 owing to the great post-war demand for passages and carriage of freight to and from the home country. This lasted until the early Fifties. Today, the company maintains a large fleet on worldwide operations.

Europe-Canada Line was formed by Holland-America Line in 1955 for a specific German service as well as student transport. It was closed down as a subsidiary in 1966.

French Line started its transatlantic service in 1864, a link that survived until 1974. French Line passenger interests remain, however, in Mediterranean and North African car-ferry services; there is a cargo-ship fleet as well.

Furness-Warren Line began as George Warren & Company in 1865. It was acquired by Furness Withy & Company Limited in 1912 and thus the styling of the name as Furness-Warren. Passenger services survived until 1961.

German-Atlantic Line was created in 1967 as a successor to the earlier Hamburg-Atlantic Line. It remained, although primarily interested in cruising, until 1973.

Greek Line began as the General Steam Navigation Company of Greece in 1939. A number of Panamanian subsidiaries were formed as owning companies. Operations continued until 1975 when the last ship returned to Greece and lay-up, a consequence of increased operational and fuel costs.

Grimaldi-Siosa Lines opened its occasional transatlantic service in the mid-Fifties. By 1962, it had switched completely to the Caribbean and still later to cruising only. It is currently styled simply as Siosa Lines.

Hamburg-Atlantic Line opened its Atlantic service in 1958 with a financial interest held by Home Lines. Its only ship was destroyed by fire in 1966 and the firm was reorganized as the German-Atlantic Line a year later.

Holland-America Line had its first sailing from Rotterdam to New York in 1872. The Atlantic service survived until 1971 when the Company switched to year-round cruising, mostly from American ports.

Home Lines came into being in 1946 for the immigrant runs to Central and South America and then later on the North Atlantic to Canada and New York. Liner service to Europe was discontinued in 1963 and concentration placed on year-round cruises from New York.

Incres Line, organized in 1950, spent fifteen months in the transatlantic trade before transferring completely to cruise services. It was sold to the Clipper Line of Sweden in 1964, but retained its individual identity until bankruptcy in 1975.

Italian Line was created in 1932 under the direction of Mussolini's government by combining Italy's three leading Atlantic firms: Navigazione Generale Italiana, Cosulich Line and Lloyd Sabaudo. All ships were incorporated into the new fleet, including those under construction at the time. As the original trade dwindled, the final crossing from America to Genoa and Naples took place in 1976.

Jugolinija opened its transatlantic passenger-cargo service in 1949. It continues, quite successfully, with a series of four combination ships.

Khedivial Mail Line was Egypt's only transatlantic passenger-ship line after World War II. It survived until 1960, when the company was realigned as the United Arab Maritime Company. The Khedivial Mail name and regular passenger services seem to have disappeared at that time.

Lauro Line was formed in 1923 as a tramp-steamer operator. However, following the war years, with the large number of immigrants and displaced persons needing transport, it established passenger services. The Atlantic trade survived only between 1953 and 1956, and thereafter emphasis was on the Australia and West Indies runs. The last regular liner-sailing to Sydney took place in 1973 and since then the company has concentrated on cruising.

National Hellenic American Line was developed as a Greek-flag subsidiary of Home Lines in 1954. The firm's only ship and the rights to its name and service were sold to Chandris Lines in 1965.

Netherlands Government had the responsibility of transporting vast numbers of immigrants, displaced persons and even students at times. Its three rather austere ships were linked to Holland-America, Nederland Line and Royal Rotterdam Lloyd for operational reasons and remained in service from 1951 until 1963.

New Zealand Shipping Company, although dating from the turn-of-the-century, did not begin calling at North American ports until the early Sixties. An eastbound transatlantic service between Port Everglades and London was available as part of the full round trip to New Zealand itself via the Panama Canal. The company discontinued its passenger runs in 1969.

North German Lloyd had its first sailing to New York in 1858 and, by 1913, had the second largest fleet in the world (Hamburg-America Line, its chief rival, had the largest). Atlantic crossings were void from the summer of 1939 until early 1955. The transatlantic trade was finally discontinued in 1971 and the company merged with Hamburg-America to create Hapag-Lloyd.

Norwegian America Line was founded in 1910, with a transatlantic service beginning three years later. Atlantic liner runs were discontinued in 1971 and the emphasis placed completely on luxury cruising.

Oranje Line was formed in 1937 but did not have a ship carrying more than twelve passengers until 1953. Its services through the St Lawrence Seaway to Chicago and the Great Lakes were quite novel, and lasted until 1964. Shortly thereafter the company went into liquidation.

P&O-Orient Lines was created by the combination of the Peninsular & Oriental Steamship Company Limited and the Orient Line, both competitors in the England-Australia trade. P&O — formed in 1837 — is one of the world's oldest existing steamship companies and possesses one of the largest merchant fleets. In 1961, P&O-Orient combined had the largest passenger-liner fleet on the high seas.

Polish Ocean Lines was also known as Gdynia-America Line and was established in 1930. It remains in passenger service at present (1980).

Royal Viking Line is one of the world's more deluxe cruising companies and was created by three Norwegian partners in 1969: Bergen Line, Norden-fjeldske and A. F. Klaveness.

Shaw Savill Line was established in 1859 and later acquired such firms as the Albion Line, the Aberdeen line and also White Star's Australian service. Its interests have always been concentrated on Australia and New Zealand. Stopovers in Florida were begun in the mid-Sixties, hence creating a transatlantic operation. In 1975, the firm sold off its last passenger ship and discontinued all of its liner services.

Sitmar Line was created primarily for immigrant services. All regular liner runs were discontinued in favour of complete cruising in the early Seventies.

Soviet Ministry of Shipping, which was known officially as Sovtorgflot, operated several passenger vessels on the Atlantic in the immediate post-war period, including the larger *Russia*. As political tensions developed, the service was suspended completely by 1948.

Spanish Line had its beginnings in 1881 but did not commence services to New York until 1900. Freighters replaced the last passenger ships in 1972.

Splosna Plovba had short-lived passenger services during the Sixties. At present it maintains a worldwide freighter operation.

Swedish American Line had its first sailing from Gothenburg to New York in 1915. North Atlantic services finished in the late Sixties and the final cruise was completed in 1975.

Turkish Maritime Lines had occasional transatlantic crossings during the Fifties but within a decade all passenger runs were confined to the Mediterranean and Black Seas.

United States Lines began in 1921, a creation of the United States Shipping Board. Services to Northern Europe lasted until 1969. Thereafter, the company engaged exclusively in container shipping.

Zim Lines was created in 1945 to carry Jewish immigrants to Palestine using whatever available tonnage. A transatlantic service began in 1953 and was finally terminated in 1967, a victim of high operational costs. Zim currently operates worldwide freighter services.

Southampton Docks in 1966: *Queen Mary* is in the centre; *Franconia* and *Andes* are in the lower portion. *Pendennis Castle* and *Caronia* are docked at the far end of the terminal (*Southern Newspapers Limited*)

New York, showing from left to right: *Berlin, Mauretania, Queen Elizabeth, Italia, Ocean Monarch and Gripsholm. Homeric* is in mid-river about to dock (*Transatlantic Steamship Conference*)

At Le Havre, *Batory, United States* (sailing) and *France* (*United States Lines*)

The Port of Bremerhaven with *Bremen* about to dock, the American troopship *General A. M. Patch* and the *United States* beyond (*North German Lloyd*)

Nieuw Amsterdam alongside the Holland-America terminal at Rotterdam (*Vincent Messina Collection*)

United States arriving at Southampton with *Queen Elizabeth* and the British troopship *Empire Windrush* in the background (*United States Lines*)

Raffaello is in the distance in this view of Genoa (*Italian Line*)

Atlantic arriving in New York on her maiden voyage in June 1958 (*Frank O. Braynard Collection*)

American Banner Lines

ATLANTIC

Service New York to Zeebrugge (Belgium) and Amsterdam.
Particulars 14,138 tons gross; 564x76x28ft.
Builders Sun Shipbuilding & Drydock Company, Chester, Pennsylvania, 1953.
Machinery Steam turbines geared to single screw; service speed 20 knots.
Capacity 40 first class, 860 tourist class.
Notes Former freighter rebuilt as a passenger ship.

1953, 1 July Launched as the 'Mariner' class freighter *Badger Mariner* for the United States Maritime Administration.
1953 Oct Entered service; tonnage 9,214.
1953-7 Worldwide cargo service.
1957 Sold to American Banner Lines (Arnold Bernstein), US flag, renamed *Atlantic*. Rebuilt as a passenger ship by Ingalls Shipbuilding Yard, Pascagoula, Mississippi.
1958, 11 June Entered transatlantic passenger service.
1959 Oct Final American Banner sailing; laid-up at Bethlehem Steel Yard, Hoboken. Sold to American Export Lines (qv).

LA GUARDIA

Service New York to Naples and Genoa; later extended to Palermo, Piraeus and Haifa.
Particulars 17,951 tons gross; 622x76x26ft.
Builders Federal Shipbuilding & Drydock Company, Kearny, New Jersey, 1944.
Machinery Steam turbines geared to twin screw; service speed 20 knots.
Capacity 157 first class, 452 tourist class.
Notes Former troopship rebuilt as a passenger ship; more money spent on this vessel in rebuildings and conversions than any other liner ever built.

1944, 6 Aug Launched as *General W.P. Richardson*, US Government troopship (5,200 troops, 475 crew). Original intention was to name her *General R.M. Blatchford*. Cost $7 million.
1944, 2 Nov Commissioned for active duty.
1946 Feb Transferred to the US Army for further trooping.
1948 Mar Declared surplus and laid-up. Chartered to American Export Lines, who offered to refit the ship for regular liner service. Rebuilt at Ingalls Shipbuilding Yard, Pascagoula, Mississippi; cost $5 million.
1949, 27 May First transatlantic sailing as *La Guardia*.
1951, 13 Dec Returned to the Maritime Commission as 'uneconomic'.
1952 Made some trans-Pacific trooping voyages during the Korean War.
1952 Nov Laid-up in the James River, Virginia Reserve Fleet.
1956 Sold to Hawaiian Textron Lines for $3.5 million; refitted for an additional $4 million and renamed *Leilani*. San Francisco-Honolulu cruise service; 650 one-class passengers.
1959 Jan Laid-up again.
1960 Sold to American President Lines for $3.2 million; sent to Puget Sound Bridge and Drydock Company at Seattle. Rebuilt for a further $10 million; renamed *President Roosevelt*.
1962, 10 May Maiden trans-Pacific cruise from San Francisco for American President; 456 first-class passengers; tonnage listed as 18,920.
1970 Mar Sold to Solon Navigation S/A, Greece (Chandris Group), for $1.8 million; renamed *Atlantis*. Rebuilt at Perama, Greece: tonnage increased to 24,458 and capacity boosted to 1,092 one-class.
1971 June Maiden cruise, New York-Nassau.
1972, 31 Jan Sold to Eastern Steamship Lines, delivery in November.
1972 Apr Was to have been chartered to Cunard for New York-Bermuda service but this never materialized.
1972 Nov Renamed *Emerald Seas*, Panamanian flag, Miami-Nassau-Freeport service; 962 one-class passengers. Owned by Ares Shipping Corporation and operated by Eastern Steamship Lines of Miami; still in service.

The former troopship *La Guardia* as she appeared after her 1949 rebuilding (*Frank O. Braynard Collection*)

Numerous refits later, the same ship as *Emerald Seas* in 1973 (*Eastern Steamship Lines*)

The *Excalibur* at New York in the 1950s (*American Export Lines*)

The same ship as the *Oriental Jade* in 1971 (*Orient Overseas Line*)

American Export Lines

EXCALIBUR

Service New York to Barcelona, Marseilles, Naples, Alexandria, Beirut, Iskenderun (Turkey), Latakia, Beirut, Alexandria, Piraeus, Naples, Genoa, Marseilles, Barcelona and return to New York. Round trip of 47 days; routing later modified.
Particulars 9,644 tons gross; 473x66x27ft.
Builders Bethlehem Steel Company, Sparrows Point, Maryland, 1944.
Machinery Steam turbines geared to single screw; service speed 17 knots.
Capacity 125 first-class passengers.
Notes These four sisters were known as the 'Four Aces'.

1944 Commissioned as the transport USS *Duchess* for the US Navy.
1944-7 Military work.
1947-8 Purchased by American Export Lines and underwent major refit; renamed *Excalibur*.
1948, 24 Sept Maiden voyage from New York to the Mediterranean.
1950, 27 June Rammed Danish freighter *Colombia* in New York harbour; heavy damages; *Excalibur* grounded on Gowanus Flats. Later repaired.
1965 Sold to Atlantic Far East Lines (C.Y.Tung Group), Liberian flag; renamed *Oriental Jade*. San Francisco-Far East service.
1974, 22 Jan Arrived at Kaohsiung, Taiwan for scrapping.

EXCAMBION

Service New York to Barcelona, Marseilles, Naples, Alexandria, Beirut, Iskenderun, Latakia, Beirut, Alexandria, Piraeus, Naples, Genoa, Marseilles, Barcelona and return to New York. Round trip of 47 days.
Particulars 9,644 tons gross; 473x66x27ft.
Builders Bethlehem Steel Company, Sparrows Point, Maryland, 1944.
Machinery Steam turbines geared to single screw; service speed 17 knots.
Capacity 125 first-class passengers.

1944, 16 Dec Commissioned as USS *Queens* as a US Navy transport.
1944-7 Government work.
1947 Sold to American Export Lines; renamed *Excambion* and began major refit.
1948, 3 Dec Departed from New York on maiden Mediterranean cruise.
1959 Laid-up in the Hudson River Reserve Fleet.
1965 Transferred to Texas Aviation & Maritime University at Galveston. Refitted as a cadet training ship; renamed *Texas Clipper*.

The *Exeter* with her American Export funnel colours in 1962 (*Alex Duncan*)

EXETER

Service New York to Barcelona, Marseilles, Naples, Alexandria, Beirut, Iskenderun, Latakia, Beirut, Alexandria, Piraeus, Naples, Genoa, Marseilles, Barcelona and return to New York. Round trip of 47 days; ports-of-call later altered.
Particulars 9,644 tons gross; 473x66x27ft.
Builders Bethlehem Steel Company, Sparrows Point, Maryland, 1944.
Machinery Steam turbines geared to single screw; service speed 17 knots.
Capacity 125 first-class passengers.

1945, 20 Jan Commissioned as USS *Shelby*, attack transport for the US Navy.
1945-7 Military duties.
1947 Purchased by American Export Lines; rebuilt and renamed *Exeter*.
1948, 1 Dec Maiden sailing from New York to the Mediterranean.
1964 Laid-up at New York.
1965 Sold to Atlantic Far East Lines (C.Y.Tung Group), Liberian flag, renamed *Oriental Pearl*. Assigned to new passenger-cargo service between California and the Far East.
1974 Scrapped at Kaohsiung, Taiwan.

The final departure from New York of the student accommodation ship *Stevens* (ex-*Exochorda*) for scrapping at Chester, Pennsylvania (*Stevens Institute of Technology*)

EXOCHORDA

Service New York to Barcelona, Marseilles, Naples, Alexandria, Beirut, Iskenderun, Latakia, Beirut, Alexandria, Piraeus, Naples, Genoa, Marseilles, Barcelona and return to New York. Round trip of 47 days.
Particulars 9,644 tons gross; 473x66x27ft.
Builders Bethlehem Steel Company, Sparrows Point, Maryland, 1944.
Machinery Steam turbines geared to single screw; service speed 17 knots.
Capacity 125 first-class passengers.

1944 Commissioned as USS *Dauphin*, US Navy attack transport.
1944-7 Military work.
1947 Sold to American Export Lines; renamed *Exochorda* and rebuilt.
1948, 2 Nov Maiden voyage to the Mediterranean.
1959 Laid-up in Reserve Fleet in Hudson River, New York.
1967 Removed from Reserve Fleet; sold to Stevens Institute of Technology, Hoboken, New Jersey. Converted to a floating student dormitory by Bethlehem Steel Company, Hoboken; renamed *Stevens*. Later moved to permanent berth on the Hudson River.
1975 Aug Towed to Chester, Pennsylvania for scrapping.
1979 Mar Half-scrapped ship towed back to New York; completely scrapped at Kearny, New Jersey.

INDEPENDENCE

Service New York to Algeciras, Cannes, Genoa and Naples; also cruising to the Caribbean and Mediterranean.
Particulars 30,293 tons gross; 683x89x30ft.

Independence as photographed in 1959 (*American Export Lines*)

As the *Oceanic Independence*, she cruised from Capetown and Durban in 1975 (*Michael D. J. Lennon*)

Builders Bethlehem Steel Company, Quincy, Massachusetts, 1951.
Machinery Steam turbines geared to twin screw; service speed 23 knots.
Capacity 295 first class, 375 cabin class and 330 tourist class. Hawaiian cruise capacity listed as 721, all first class (1,021 maximum).
Notes When new, the *Independence* was the fastest American liner.

1949, 19 Mar Keel laid down.
1950, 3 June Launched.
1951, 11 Feb Maiden sailing from New York on a 53-day Mediterranean cruise.
1959 Feb-Mar Extensive refit at Newport News Shipyard; 110 first-class berths added.
1960 Repainted with white hull.
1968 Operated by Fugazy Travel Service and repainted in bright colours for cruising; New York-Caribbean and Mediterranean cruises proved uneconomical.
1969 Mar Laid-up at Baltimore.
1974 Mar Sold to Atlantic Far East Lines (C.Y.Tung Group), Liberian flag; renamed *Oceanic Independence*. Sailed to Hong Kong and refitted for further cruising.
1975 Cruising from Capetown; 950 one-class passengers.
1976, 19 Jan Laid-up at Hong Kong.
1977 Mar Renamed *Sea-Luck I*. Remained idle; plan to become a floating hotel in the Middle East never materialized.
1979 Aug Rumoured return to American flag for California-Hawaiian Islands cruising.
1979 Dec Commenced refit at Kobe, Japan, in preparation for Hawaiian island cruise service as *Oceanic Independence*.
1980 June Placed under the American flag for American Hawaii Cruises.
1980, 21 June First weekly 7-day cruise from Honolulu.

Constitution shown after 1960 with a white hull (*American Export Lines*)

As the *Oceanic Constitution*, owned by C. Y. Tung but with her original funnel colours, she was laid-up near Hong Kong (*Michael D. J. Lennon*)

CONSTITUTION

Service New York to Algeciras, Cannes, Genoa and Naples; also cruising in the Caribbean and Mediterranean.
Particulars 30,293 tons gross; 683x89x30ft.
Builders Bethlehem Steel Company, Quincy, Massachusetts, 1951.
Machinery Steam turbines geared to twin screw; service speed 23 knots.
Capacity 295 first class, 375 cabin class and 330 tourist class.

1949, 12 July Keel laid down.
1950, 16 Sept Launched.
1951, 21 June Maiden voyage from New York to the Mediterranean.
1959 Jan-Feb Extensive refit at Newport News, Virginia: 110 first-class berths added.
1959, 1 Mar Collided outside New York Harbour with the Norwegian tanker *Jalanta*; tanker lost 135ft of her bow section. *Constitution* damaged and repaired in Brooklyn.
1960 Repainted with white hull.
1968 Cruising only.
1968 Sept Laid-up at Jacksonville, Florida.
1974 Mar Sold to Atlantic Far East Line (C.Y.Tung Group), Liberian flag; renamed *Oceanic Constitution*.
1974, 26 Apr Left Jacksonville under tow.
1974, 4 Aug Arrived at Hong Kong and laid-up.
1980 Aug Rumoured to be under consideration for California-Hawaii cruise service for America Hawaii Cruises, US flag. Intention would be for thorough refit and possible conversion to diesel propulsion; reintroduction would be in 1982.

Atlantic in New York Harbour in a unique photograph in 1960 that shows her without all but one of her lifeboats (*Frank O. Braynard Collection*)

As *Universe Campus*, she was used as an educational cruiseship during the early 1970s (*Michael Cassar*)

ATLANTIC

Service New York to Algeciras, Naples, Messina, Piraeus and Haifa; periodic alterations in scheduling; off-season cruising to the Caribbean.
Particulars 14,138 tons gross; 564x76x28ft.
Builders Sun Shipbuilding & Drydock Company, Chester, Pennsylvania, 1953.
Machinery Steam turbines geared to single screw; service speed 20 knots.
Capacity 40 first class and 840 tourist class.
Notes Former freighter rebuilt as a passenger ship. After refit in 1960, this ship had the largest outdoor swimming pool afloat.

1953, 1 July Launched as freighter *Badger Mariner*; see *Atlantic*, American Banner Lines.
1959 Oct Purchased by American Export Lines; refitted by Sun Shipbuilding & Drydock Company, Chester, Pennsylvania.
1960, 16 May Maiden sailing for American Export, New York-Mediterranean.
1965 Apr Restyled as an 'all-tourist ship' (840 one-class passengers).
1967 Oct Withdrawn and laid-up at Brooklyn.
1968 May Planned to become trade ship displaying American merchandise; to be renamed *Atlantic World Trade Ship*. Scheme never materialized.
1969 Mar Transferred to Baltimore; still laid-up.
1971 Sold to Seawise Foundations Inc (C.Y.Tung Group); Liberian flag; sale price $2.4 million. Renamed *Universe Campus*; refitted as an educational cruiseship.
1971 Sept Commenced first 'educational cruise' with students and teachers.
1976 Renamed *Universe*; laid-up at San Francisco.
1977 Began regular cruising from North American ports.

The nuclear-powered merchant ship *Savannah* during her maiden arrival at Southampton (*American Export Lines*)

SAVANNAH

Service Goodwill demonstration voyages from New York to ports around the world; later, New York-Mediterranean and North European service.
Particulars 13,599 tons gross; 595x78x29ft.
Builders New York Shipbuilding Company, Camden, New Jersey, 1958-62.
Machinery Nuclear reactor plus turbines geared to single screw; service speed 20 knots.
Capacity 60 first-class passengers.
Notes World's first nuclear-powered merchant ship.

1958, 22 May Keel laid; sponsored by Mrs Richard Nixon.
1959, 21 July Launched by Mrs Dwight Eisenhower.
1961 Dec-1962 Apr Special extended sea trials; total cost $53 million.
1962 May Assigned to States Marine Lines for management; owned by the US Government. Sailed on 'goodwill demonstration' voyages to Germany, England, Ireland, Holland, Belgium, Denmark, Sweden, Norway, Greece, Portugal, Spain, Italy and France.
1964 Assigned to New York-Mediterranean service.
1965 Aug Management transferred to American Export (FAST = First Atomic Ship Transport).
1966 Ceased carrying passengers.
1969 Feb Offered for charter.
1970 Laid-up at Galveston, Texas.
1972 Laid-up at Savannah, Georgia; later moved to Charleston, South Carolina.

President Monroe sailing from San Francisco (*American President Lines*)

American President Lines

PRESIDENT MONROE

Service Continuous around-the-world sailings: New York to Cristobal, Balboa, Acapulco, San Francisco, Honolulu, Yokohama, Kobe, Hong Kong, Singapore, Penang, Colombo, Cochin, Bombay, Karachi, Suez, Port Said, Alexandria, Naples, Marseilles, Genoa, Leghorn and New York. Transatlantic passengers carried on the westbound Mediterranean-New York portion.
Particulars 9,255 tons gross; 492x70x27ft.
Builders Newport News Shipbuilding & Drydock Company, Newport News, Virginia, 1940.
Machinery Steam turbines geared to single screw; service speed 16.5 knots.
Capacity 96 first-class passengers.

1940, 28 Dec Maiden voyage New York-Panama-California-Bombay-Capetown-New York (3 round-trip voyages).
1941 Dec Chartered to War Shipping Administration; military work.
1943 July-1946 Nov Chartered to the US Navy.
1946, 25 Nov First post-war world cruise.
1965 Dec Withdrawn from American President service; laid-up.
1966 Sold to White Star Shipping & Trading Company (John S. Latsis Line), Greek flag; sale price $650,000; renamed *Marianna V*. General Mediterranean and tramping services.
1969, 26 June Arrived at Hong Kong for scrapping.

President Polk bound for the Orient (*American President Lines*)

PRESIDENT POLK

Service Continuous around-the-world sailings. Ports same as *President Monroe*
Particulars 9,260 tons gross; 492x70x27ft.
Builders Newport News Shipbuilding & Drydock Company, Newport News, Virginia, 1940.
Machinery Steam turbines geared to single screw; service speed 16.5 knots.
Capacity 96 first-class passengers.

1940, 6 Nov Maiden voyage New York-Panama-California.
1941 Dec-1943 Sept Chartered to US War Shipping Administration; military service.
1943 Sept-1946 Aug Chartered to the US Navy.
1946, 13 Aug First post-war world cruise.
1965 Dec Withdrawn from service and briefly laid-up. Sold to Ganderos del Mar S/A, Liberian flag; sale price $650,000; renamed *Gaucho Martin Fierro*; refitted as a cattle carrier.
1966 Renamed *Minotaurus*.
1980 No longer listed as sailing; presumed scrapped.

The *Arosa Kulm* as rebuilt from the passenger-cargo ship *American Banker* (*Alex Duncan*)

Arosa Line

AROSA KULM

Service Montreal (from Halifax in the winter) to Southampton, Zeebrugge and Bremerhaven; numerous alterations in schedule including occasional sailings to New York.
Particulars 8,929 tons gross; 448x58x36ft.
Builders American International Shipbuilding Corporation, Hog Island, Pennsylvania, 1920.
Machinery Steam turbines geared to single screw; service speed 14.5 knots.
Capacity 46 first class and 919 tourist class; later changed to 20 first and 945 tourist, and finally to 30 first and 802 tourist.
Notes Former freighter rebuilt as a passenger vessel; first Arosa Line ship.

1920 Launched by King Albert of Belgium as the Hog Island-type transport *Cantigny*.
1924 Sold to United States Lines and rebuilt as the combination ship *American Banker*; 65 one-class passengers (later increased to 85). New York-London service.
1940 Owing to American neutrality and the eruption of war in Europe, ship transferred to Antwerp Navigation Company; renamed *Ville d'Anvers*.
1940-6 War service as a freighter.
1946 Returned to United States Lines then to Luckenbach Line; placed under Honduran flag. Transferred to Sociedad Naviera Transatlantic, Panamanian flag; rebuilt as the immigrant ship *City of Athens*.
1947 Seized for debt and auctioned-off to Panamanian Lines; renamed *Protea*; emigrant services.
1949 Ownership changed to Cia de Operaziones Maritima, Panama; Australian immigrant sailings from Mediterranean ports.
1951 Chartered to Incres Line for three transatlantic sailings Antwerp-Plymouth-Montreal. Then sold to Arosa Line and rebuilt at Bremerhaven for tourist service; renamed *Arosa Kulm*.
1952 Mar Opened Arosa Line service to Montreal.
1958 Dec Seized for debt at Plymouth, England.
1959, 7 May Arrived at Bruges for scrapping.

AROSA SUN

Service Bremerhaven, Le Havre, Southampton to Quebec City and/or Montreal. Periodic other voyages to New York and off-season cruising.
Particulars 20,126 tons gross; 598x68x33ft.
Builders Ateliers et Chantiers de la Loire, St Nazaire, France, 1930.
Machinery Sulzer-type diesels geared to twin screw; service speed 16.5 knots.
Capacity 100 first class and 949 tourist class.

1929, 17 Dec Launched.
1931, 26 Feb Left Marseilles on maiden voyage to the Far East via Suez as *Felix Roussel* for Messageries Maritimes, French flag.
1936 Lengthened (from 568 to 598ft) and re-powered at La Ciotat, France.
1940-6 Trooping for the Allies; managed by the Bibby Line, British flag.
1946, 15 Apr Decommissioned at Durban; returned to Messageries Maritimes.
1948 June-1950 Sept Major refit at Dunkirk: single stack replaced former two. Returned to Marseilles-Far East service.
1955 Apr Sold to Arosa Line for $3.5 million; refitted at Trieste.
1955 July Arosa Line maiden voyage: Trieste-Palermo-Naples-Lisbon-New York-Quebec City-Le Havre-Southampton-Bremerhaven.
1955 Aug Thereafter sailings from Bremerhaven to Canada.
1958, 15 Mar Engine-room explosion off Colombia during a Caribbean cruise.
1958 Dec Arrested for debt at Bremerhaven; laid-up.
1959 Reportedly sold to Grimaldi-Siosa Lines; never materialized.
1960 Sept Sold to Kon Nederlandsche Hoogovens & Staalfabricken, Holland.
1961 Feb Used as a permanently moored accommodation ship at IJmuiden, Holland.
1963, 9 Apr Damaged in fire.
1974, 28 Mar Arrived in Bilbao for scrapping, under tow from IJmuiden.

Arosa Sun during her maiden arrival at New York in July 1955 (*Alex Duncan*)

The same ship as an accommodation centre at IJmuiden, Holland, during the 1960s (*Alex Duncan*)

AROSA STAR

Service Bremerhaven, Le Havre, Southampton, Quebec City and/or Montreal. Periodic changes in scheduling including sailings to Halifax or New York and cruises.
Particulars 9,070 tons gross; 466x60x23ft.
Builders Bethlehem Steel Company, Quincy, Massachusetts, 1931.
Machinery Steam turbines geared to single screw; service speed 15 knots.
Capacity 38 first class and 768 tourist class.

1931-41 Cruise and passenger service for New York & Puerto Rico Steamship Company as *Borinquen* between New York, San Juan and Ciudad Trujillo; 261 first-class and 96 second-class passengers. US flag.
1942-6 Government trooping.
1946-9 Reconditioned and returned to Caribbean service for Agwilines.
1949 Sold to Bull Line; renamed *Puerto Rico*. Continued in service.
1953 Mar Laid-up at Brooklyn.
1954 Jan Sold to Arosa Line, Panamanian flag. Refitted at Bremerhaven for $1million: capacity increased to 806; renamed *Arosa Star*.
1954, 18 May Maiden sailing for Arosa Line, Bremerhaven-Quebec City.
1958, 7 Dec Seized at Bermuda for debt.
1959 Sold to McCormick Shipping Corporation, Panama, for $510,000; renamed *Bahama Star*. Refitted at Jacksonville for Miami-Nassau service.
1968 Nov Withdrawn; laid-up.
1969 Sold to Western Steamship Company, Panama; renamed *La Janelle*.
1970, 13 Apr Became a total loss during a hurricane; beached at Port Hueneme, California, and later scrapped on the spot. It had been intended that she would become a permanently moored floating hotel.

Arosa Star as she appeared in 1954 after rebuilding at Bremerhaven (*Alex Duncan*)

The same ship, as *La Janelle*, wrecked at Port Hueneme, California, in April 1970 (*J. F. Rodriguez*)

Arosa Sky was flagship of the Arosa Line fleet for little more than a year (*Herbert G. Frank Jr Collection*)

AROSA SKY

Service Bremerhaven. Le Havre. Southampton. Halifax and New York. Crusing and charter sailings also.
Particulars 17,408 tons gross; 594x75x26ft.
Builders Société Provençale de Constructions Navales, La Ciotat, France, 1939-49.
Machinery Sulzer-type diesels geared to triple screw; service speed 21 knots.
Capacity 64 first class and 834 tourist class.

1939 Keel laid; then interrupted by the war.
1944, 16 June Launched as the *Maréchal Petain*.
1944 Aug Sunk by the Nazi forces in retreat.
1946 Raised and towed to Toulon for completion; renamed *La Marseillaise*.
1949, 18 Aug Maiden voyage for Messageries Maritimes on Marseilles-Far East service.
1957 Feb Sold to Arosa Line, Panamanian flag, for $6.5 million. Renamed *Arosa Sky*; refitted.
1957, 10 May Maiden voyage for Arosa Line; Bremerhaven-Le Havre-Southampton-Halifax-New York.
1958, 8 Jan Fire in passenger cabins off Wilmington, North Carolina, during cruise.
1958 Oct Sold to Costa Line, Italian flag, for $8 million; renamed *Bianca C*.
1958-9 Major refit: tonnage increased to 18,427
1959 Entered Genoa-West Indies service; also cruising from New York to the Caribbean.
1961, 22 Oct Gutted by fire at Grenada, British West Indies; sank in deep water on 24 October.

Alexandr Pushkin at Bremerhaven (*Engler-Luftbild*)

Baltic Steamship Company

ALEXANDR PUSHKIN

Service Leningrad, Bremerhaven, London, Le Havre to Montreal. Service available in April through October; occasional cruising.
Particulars 19,860 tons gross; 577x77x27ft.
Builders Mathias-Thesen Werft Shipyard, Wismar, East Germany, 1965.
Machinery Sulzer-type diesels geared to twin screw; service speed 20 knots.
Capacity 86 first class and 580 tourist class; later changed to 680 one-class passengers.
Notes First Soviet passenger liner to provide a regular Atlantic service since the late Forties and the first regular Soviet passenger service to Canada.

1964, 26 May Launched.
1965 June Maiden cruise.
1966, 18 Apr Maiden transatlantic crossing to Montreal.
1974-5 Improved for further cruising; tonnage listed as 20,502.
1981 Transatlantic service temporarily discontinued; cruising from European ports only.

The *Pushkin's* sistership *Mikhail Lermontov* anchored at Valletta, Malta, during a cruise (*Michael Cassar*)

MIKHAIL LERMONTOV

Service Leningrad, Bremerhaven, London, Le Havre to New York during the May through October period. Winter cruising.
Particulars 19,872 tons gross; 578x77x27ft.
Builders Mathias-Thesen Werft Shipyard, Wismar, East Germany, 1971.
Machinery Sulzer-type diesels geared to twin screw; service speed 20 knots.
Capacity 700 one-class passengers.
Notes The first Soviet liner to offer regular service to New York since the late Forties.

1970, 31 Dec Launched.
1972 Apr Maiden voyage: cruise from Bremerhaven to the Canary Islands.
1972, 19 June Arrived at Montreal on first transatlantic crossing.
1973 May Began sailings to New York.
1980 Sept-Oct Refitted to be more suitable for one-class cruising.
1981 Transatlantic service temporarily discontinued; cruising from European ports only.

Empress of France with her new domed funnels fitted in 1959 (*Canadian Pacific Steamships*)

Canadian Pacific Steamships

EMPRESS OF FRANCE

Service Liverpool and Greenock to Quebec City and Montreal (to Saint John, NB, in winter).
Particulars 20,448 tons gross; 601x75x27ft.
Builders John Brown & Company Limited, Clydebank, Scotland, 1928.
Machinery Steam turbines geared to twin screw; service speed 18 knots.
Capacity 400 first class and 300 tourist class. After 1958-9 refit: 218 first class and 482 tourist class.

1928, 24 Jan Launched.
1928, 1 June Maiden voyage Liverpool-Montreal as *Duchess of Bedford*.
1928-39 Summer service Liverpool-Belfast-Greenock-Quebec City-Montreal; winter cruises from New York to the West Indies and Mediterranean.
1933 Jan Four-months charter to Furness-Bermuda Line for New York-Bermuda sailings.
1939 Aug Trooping, first voyage Liverpool-Bombay.
1939-47 War service.
1948, 1 Sept Returned to Liverpool-Montreal service as *Empress of France* (original intention was to rename her as *Empress of India*).
1959 Jan Given new streamlined funnels; accommodation changes.
1960, 7 Dec Completed 338th and final Canadian Pacific voyage at Liverpool; sold for scrap at Newport, Monmouthshire.

Empress of Canada as photographed in 1948 (*Canadian Pacific Steamships*)

EMPRESS OF CANADA

Service Liverpool and Greenock to Quebec City and Montreal (to Saint John, NB, in winter).
Particulars 20,235 tons gross; 600x75x27ft.
Builders John Brown & Company Limited, Clydebank, Scotland, 1928.
Machinery Steam turbines geared to twin screw; service speed 18 knots.
Capacity 400 first class and 300 tourist class.

1928 June Launched; named *Duchess of Richmond*.
1929, 15 Mar Departed Liverpool on maiden voyage to Saint John, New Brunswick. Thereafter service to Quebec City and Montreal, and winter cruising from New York.
1939-46 Trooping.
1946 May Commenced major refit; renamed *Empress of Canada*.
1947, 16 July Left Liverpool on post-war maiden voyage to Quebec City and Montreal.
1953, Jan 25 Gutted by fire and sunk at Liverpool.
1954, 6 Mar Refloated.
1954, 1 Sept Left Liverpool under tow for La Spezia, Italy; scrapped.

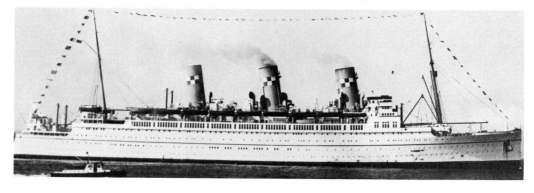

Empress of Scotland in wartime grey in 1945 (*Michael Cassar*)

EMPRESS OF SCOTLAND

Service Liverpool and Greenock to Quebec City (later extended to Montreal). Winter cruising from New York to the West Indies.
Particulars 26,313 tons gross; 666x83x31ft.
Builders Fairfield Shipbuilding & Engineering Company, Glasgow, Scotland, 1930.
Machinery Steam turbines geared to twin screw; service speed 21 knots.
Capacity 458 first class and 250 tourist class.
Notes Fastest liner in Pacific service 1930-9.

1929, 17 Dec Launched; named *Empress of Japan*.
1930 June Special maiden sailing from Liverpool to Quebec City.
1930 Aug Southampton to Vancouver via Suez and Hong Kong, thence regular trans-Pacific service between Vancouver and the Far East.
1931 Apr Record run from Yokohama to Victoria in 7 days, 20 hours, 16 minutes.
1939 Aug Requisitioned for war duty as a troopship.
1942 Oct Renamed *Empress of Scotland* prompted by Japan's entry into the war.
1948 Released from war service; commenced reconditioning.
1950, 9 May Maiden post-war sailing from Liverpool to Quebec City.
1951 Nov Carried Princess Elizabeth and Prince Philip from Portugal Cove, NF to Liverpool.
1952 May Masts shortened by 40ft so as to proceed to Montreal.
1957, 8 Nov Final Canadian Pacific sailing.
1957 Dec Laid-up at Liverpool, then at Belfast.
1958 Jan Sold to Hamburg-Atlantic Line, West German flag, tor £1 million; provisionally renamed *Scotland*, then formally renamed *Hanseatic* (qv).

The *Empress of Scotland* dressed overall for her post-war maiden voyage in May 1950 (*Canadian Pacific Steamships*)

Empress of Australia, the former French liner *De Grasse* (*J. K. Byass*)

EMPRESS OF AUSTRALIA

Service Liverpool and Greenock to Quebec City and Montreal (to Saint John, NB, in winter).
Particulars 19,370 tons gross; 574x71x29ft.
Builders Cammell Laird & Company, Birkenhead, England, 1924.
Machinery Steam turbines geared to twin screw; service speed 16 knots.
Capacity 220 first class and 444 tourist class.

1924-53 Sailed as *De Grasse* for the French Line (qv).
1953 Mar Sold to Canadian Pacific Steamships, British flag, as emergency replacement for the fire-gutted *Empress of Canada*.
1953, 27 Apr Renamed *Empress of Australia*.
1953, 28 Apr Maiden sailing from Liverpool to Quebec City and Montreal.
1955, 5 Dec Sailed from Quebec City on final Canadian Pacific voyage.
1956, 9 Jan Departed Liverpool for Gareloch; laid-up.
1956, 15 Feb Sold to Grimaldi-Siosa Lines, Italian flag; renamed *Venezuela* for the Genoa-West Indies immigrant service. Reconditioned and tonnage adjusted to 18,567.
1960 Major refit: new bow added, increasing length to 614ft; tonnage revised to 18,769; passenger accommodation restyled as 180 first, 500 tourist and 800 third.
1962, 17 Mar Grounded at Cannes. Refloated on 16 April; beyond economic repair.
1962, 26 Aug Sold for scrap at La Spezia, Italy.

The immigrant ship *Beaverbrae*, which sailed westbound with passengers and eastbound as a cargo vessel (*Canadian Pacific Steamships*)

BEAVERBRAE

Service Westbound immigrant service only: Bremen to Saint John, NB; eastbound operations as a cargo ship.
Particulars 9,034 tons gross; 469x60x21ft.
Builders Blohm & Voss A/G, Hamburg, Germany, 1939.
Machinery Diesel electric geared to single screw; service speed 16 knots.
Capacity 773 one-class passengers.
Notes Former passenger-carrying freighter.

1938, 15 Dec Launched for Hamburg-America Line as *Huascaran* (32 passenger berths).
1939 Hamburg-West Coast of South America sailings.
1939-45 Used as a Nazi submarine depot ship.
1945 Seized by the Allied forces; transferred to Canada.
1947, 2 Sept Bought by Canadian Pacific from Canadian War Reparations Commission: rebuilt as an immigrant ship at Sorel, Quebec.
1948 Feb Renamed *Beaverbrae*.
1948, 25 Feb Commenced Bremen-Saint John, NB, service.
1948-54 Low-fare immigrant service.
1954, 1 Nov Sold to Cogedar Line, Italian flag; renamed *Aurelia* (qv).

Empress of Britain, launched by Her Majesty Queen Elizabeth II on 22 June 1955 (*Canadian Pacific Steamships*)

EMPRESS OF BRITAIN

Service Liverpool and Greenock to Quebec City and Montreal (to Saint John, NB, in winter); also cruising from New York to the West Indies.
Particulars 25,516 tons gross; 640x85x29ft.
Builders Fairfield Shipbuilding & Engineering Company, Glasgow, Scotland, 1956.
Machinery Steam turbines geared to twin screw; service speed 20 knots.
Capacity 160 first class and 894 tourist class.
Notes First British liner to be completely air-conditioned.

1953, 30 Sept Laid down.
1955, 22 June Launched by Her Majesty Queen Elizabeth II.
1956, 20 Apr Left Liverpool on maiden voyage to Montreal.
1964, 18 Feb Offered for sale; later in same month sold to Greek Line and renamed *Queen Anna Maria* (qv).

Empress of England as seen in 1957. Note the smoke deflector atop the funnel *(Canadian Pacific Steamships)*

EMPRESS OF ENGLAND

Service Liverpool and Greenock to Quebec City and Montreal (to Saint John, NB, in winter); also cruising from New York to the West Indies.
Particulars 25,585 tons gross; 640x85x29ft.
Builders Vickers-Armstrong Shipbuilders Limited, Newcastle-upon-Tyne, England, 1957.
Machinery Steam turbines geared to twin screw; service speed 20 knots.
Capacity 160 first class and 898 tourist class.

1954, 22 Dec Keel laid down; rumoured that she would be named *Empress of Wales*.
1956, 9 May Launched as *Empress of England* by Lady Eden.
1957, 18 Apr Sailed from Liverpool on maiden sailing.
1965, 8 Nov Collided with tanker *Lifjord* off Quebec City.
1968 Dec Repainted in new Canadian Pacific colours.
1970 Apr Sold to Shaw Savill Line, British flag. Intended name *Pacific Empress*, then christened *Ocean Monarch*; one voyage to Australia.
1970 Oct Given £4 million refit for cruising work; made one-class.
1971, 16 Oct Maiden cruise for Shaw Savill, 1,372 passengers; tonnage listed as 25,971.
1973 Full year of Pacific Ocean-cruising from Australian ports.
1975 June Withdrawn from service.
1975, 13 June Left Southampton for scrapping at Kaohsiung, Taiwan. Arrived at Kaohsiung on 17 July.
1975, 10 Dec Demolition began.

Empress of Canada under tow at Liverpool (*J. K. Byass*)

The same ship with the new CP colours in 1969 (*Canadian Pacific Steamships*)

EMPRESS OF CANADA

Service Liverpool and Greenock to Quebec City and Montreal; winter cruising from New York to the Caribbean and Mediterranean.
Particulars 27,284 tons gross; 650x87x29ft.
Builders Vickers-Armstrong Shipbuilders Limited, Newcastle-upon-Tyne, England, 1961.
Machinery Steam turbines geared to twin screw; service speed 20 knots.
Capacity 200 first class and 856 tourist class; 650 one-class for cruising.
Notes The last Canadian Pacific passenger liner.

1959, 27 Jan Keel laid.
1960, 10 May Launched by Mrs John Diefenbaker.
1961, 24 Apr Departed from Liverpool for Montreal on maiden voyage.
1968 Nov End of Canadian Pacific sailings from Greenock; thereafter service from Liverpool direct.
1968 Dec Repainted in new Canadian Pacific colours.
1969, 27 Nov First sailing from Southampton.
1970, 3 Sept First cruise from Montreal; to Saguenay, Boston and Bermuda (14 days).
1971, 23 Nov Withdrawn from service; termination of Canadian Pacific's transatlantic liner operations.
1971, 17 Dec Laid-up at Tilbury.
1972 Jan Sold to Carnival Cruise Lines, Panamanian flag, for $6 million; renamed *Mardi Gras*.
1972, 26 Feb Sailed from Tilbury for Miami, her new homeport for Caribbean cruising.

Queen Frederica in Chandris colours in 1966 (*Michael D. J. Lennon*)

Chandris Lines

QUEEN FREDERICA

Service Summer-season sailings between Piraeus, Messina, Naples and New York; also cruising from New York to Bermuda and the Caribbean. Periodic sailings from Southampton to Australia via Suez and full around-the-world voyages returning to Southampton via Panama.
Particulars 16,435 tons gross; 582x83x29ft.
Builders William Cramp & Sons Ship and Engine Building Company, Philadelphia, Pennsylvania. 1927.
Machinery Steam turbines geared to twin screw; service speed 21 knots.
Capacity 174 first class and 1,005 tourist-class passengers; often merged into one-class. 650 one-class for cruising from New York.
Notes Reached fiftieth year.

1927-37 Sailed as *Malolo* for Matson Navigation Company, American flag.
1937-48 Renamed *Matsonia* for Matson. Wartime service as a trooper.
1948 Sold to Home Lines, Panamanian flag. Renamed *Atlantic* (qv).
1954 Transferred to National Hellenic American Line, Greek flag; renamed *Queen Frederica* (qv).
1965 Nov Acquired by Chandris Group (Themistocles Navigation S/A); first Chandris sailing from Southampton to Australia.
1966, 21 Mar Arrived at New York on first Chandris crossing.
1967 Sept Final transatlantic crossing.
1969, 4 Nov Damaged by fire during a voyage from Villefranche to Piraeus.
1971 Laid-up on the River Dart, England.
1972, 28 Jan Aground in the River Dart; later refloated.
1973 Chartered to Sun Cruises for twenty-seven 7-day Mediterranean cruises from Cannes.
1973, 5 Nov Laid-up at Perama, Greece.
1977 May Sold to Greek shipbreakers.
1978, 1 Feb Gutted by fire at the shipbreakers yard at Eleusis.

ELLINIS

Service Periodic eastbound sailings from New York to Southanpton as part of full around-the-world voyages. Southampton, Piraeus, Port Said (or via Capetown), Fremantle, Melbourne, Sydney, Auckland, Tahiti, Panama, occasionally New York and return to Southampton; occasional cruising from Southampton and Sydney.
Particulars 24,351 tons gross; 642x79x28ft.
Builders Bethlehem Steel Corporation, Quincy, Massachusetts, 1932.
Machinery Steam turbines geared to twin screw; service speed 20 knots.
Capacity 1,642 tourist-class passengers.

1932, 18 July Launched as *Lurline*, Matson Navigation Company, US flag. Cost $8 million.
1933, 27 Jan Maiden voyage.
1933-41 San Francisco-Honolulu service.
1942-6 Wartime troopship.
1947-8 Major refit costing $21 million.
1948 Apr Resumed San Francisco-Honolulu sailings.
1963 Sept Sold to Chandris Group (Marfuerza Cia Maritima S/A), Greek flag; renamed *Ellinis*. Major refit at Smith's Dock Company, North Shields, increasing length from 632 to 642ft; passenger capacity increased from 761 to 1,642.
1963, 21 Dec Left the Tyne for Piraeus and Australia on first sailing for Chandris.
1968, 21 Oct First visit to New York for Chandris, thence to Southampton.
1969 Mar Struck by a 40ft wave in the North Atlantic during a New York-Southampton sailing.
1973 Oct Final New York-Southampton crossing; thereafter mostly cruising.
1974, 25 June Arrived at Rotterdam and had a turbine replaced by one from her former sister *Homeric* (ex-*Mariposa*), which had been sold for scrap in late 1973.
1975 Dec Based at Capetown for winter cruising.
1977 Ownership transferred to Australia Line S/A (Chandris Group), still Greek flag.
1981 Summer Mediterranean cruising from Genoa; laid-up during winter season.

The Matson cruiseship *Lurline* as she appeared during the 1930s (*Matson Navigation Company*)

After rebuilding in 1963, the *Lurline* was renamed *Ellinis* for Chandris Lines (*B. Reeves*)

AUSTRALIS

Service Eastbound sailings from Port Everglades to Southampton and occasionally to Rotterdam and Bremerhaven as part of continuous around-the-world service; Bremerhaven, Rotterdam, Southampton, Casablanca, Las Palmas, Capetown (or through the Mediterranean via Gibraltar, Naples, Malta, Piraeus, Port Said and Aden), Fremantle, Melbourne, Sydney, Auckland, Suva, Tahiti, Acapulco, Balboa, Cristobal, Port Everglades and Southampton; three-month round trip.
Particulars 34,449 tons gross; 723x93x32ft.
Builders Newport News Shipbuilding & Drydock Company, Newport News, Virginia, 1940.
Machinery Steam turbines geared to twin screw; service speed 20-2 knots.
Capacity 2,258 one-class passengers.
Notes Largest passenger capacity of any equivalent liner in the world at the time.

1940-64 Service as *America* (qv) for United States Lines and during the war as troopship USS *West Point*.
1964 Nov Sold to Okeania S/A (Chandris Group), Panamanian flag; renamed *Australis*. Passenger berths increased from 1,046 to 2,258 during major refit at Piraeus.
1965, 20 Aug Maiden voyage from Piraeus to Sydney.
1965 Oct Commenced around-the-world service.
1968 Repainted with grey hull (it had been white); subsequently transferred to Greek flag.
1970, 22 Oct Damaged by galley fire at sea during sailing from Auckland to Suva.
1977, 18 Nov Departed from Southampton on final voyage to Australia.
1978 Jan Laid-up at Timaru, New Zealand. Sold for $5 million to America Cruise Lines (also called Venture Cruise Lines); continued under Greek flag; renamed *America*.
1978 May Sailed to New York for new owners.
1978, 30 June Sailed from New York on first short cruise; unsuccessful. Arrested for debt on 8 July.
1978, 28 Aug Auctioned-off by US District Court and resold to Chandris Group for $1 million; sailed to Perama and laid-up.
1979 Mar Renamed *Italis*; reconditioned and forward funnel removed.
1979 Apr Mediterranean cruising; later in the year laid-up.
1980 Apr Reportedly sold to Noga Corporation, Swiss-based, for use as an African-based hotel ship; intended reconversion to cost $10 million.

Australis as photographed during her maiden voyage for Chandris Lines in August 1965 (*Alex Duncan*)

With both mainmast and forward funnel removed, she was renamed *Italis* early in 1979 (*Michael Cassar*)

Kenya Castle was fitted with a domed funnel during the 1960s (Union Castle Line)

The same ship, which was thoroughly rebuilt as the Amerikanis in 1967-8 (Chandris Lines)

AMERIKANIS

Service Piraeus, Messina, Naples and Gibraltar to New York. Cruising from New York and Boston to the Caribbean and Bermuda.
Particulars 19,377 tons gross; 576x74x28ft.
Builders Harland & Wolff Limited, Belfast, Northern Ireland, 1952.
Machinery Steam turbines geared to twin screw; service speed 19 knots.
Capacity 910 passengers in first and tourist class.

1951, 21 June Launched as Kenya Castle for Union Castle Line, London.
1952, 4 Apr Departed from London on maiden cruise around Africa.
1961 May-July Major refit: given dome on funnel.
1967, 22 Apr Laid-up on River Blackwater, England. Later sold to National Hellenic American Line S/A (Chandris Group), Greek flag; renamed Amerikanis.
1967, 12 Aug Arrived at Piraeus for rebuilding.
1968, 8 Aug Left Piraeus on maiden voyage to New York.
1970 Mostly cruising.
1973, 26 July Struck submerged object off Bermuda; damaged and repaired.
1975 Caribbean cruising from San Juan in winter; in the Mediterranean from Genoa in summer.
1980 May Commenced summer cruising from Amsterdam to the North Cape and Scandinavia.
1981 Transferred to Costa Line management for year-round Miami-Bahamas service; 3- and 4-day cruises.

Aurelia was modernized in 1958-9 and the mast moved to a position above the bridge (*Alex Duncan*)

Cogedar Line

AURELIA

Service Mostly summer-season student sailings between New York, Le Havre and Southampton; otherwise on Bremerhaven, Rotterdam, Southampton, Port Said, Suez, Aden, Fremantle, Melbourne and Sydney service.
Particulars 10,480 tons gross; 487x60x21ft.
Builders Blohm & Voss Shipbuilders A/G, Hamburg, Germany, 1939.
Machinery MAN-type diesels geared to single screw; service speed 17 knots.
Capacity 1,124 tourist-class passengers.
Notes Former passenger-carrying freighter rebuilt as a passenger ship.

1938-47 Known as *Huascaran* for Hamburg-America Line.
1947-54 Sailed as *Beaverbrae* for Canadian Pacific Steamships (qv).
1954, 1 Nov Purchased from Canadian Pacific Steamships by Cogedar Line, Italian flag; renamed *Aurelia*.
1954 Nov-1955 May Rebuilt at Monfalcone; capacity increased from 773 to 1,124 passenger berths.
1955 May Commenced Australian immigrant service from Italian ports.
1958-9 Original diesel-electric drive replaced by MAN diesels; tonnage revised from 10,022 to 10,480.
1959 Commenced Australian sailings from Bremerhaven, Rotterdam and Southampton.
1960-7 Periodic summer-season transatlantic sailings to/from New York.
1968, 23 Sept Final round-trip sailing from Rotterdam and Southampton to Australia. Extensive refit followed; 470 one-class cruise passengers.
1969, 12 Jan Commenced Southampton-Canary Islands cruise service.
1970 May Sold to International Cruises S/A (Chandris Group), Greek flag; renamed *Romanza* for Mediterranean and Black Sea cruising.
1977 Transferred to Panamanian flag by Chandris.
1979 Transferred by Chandris Group to Amadones Romanza S/A, Panamanian flag; still under Chandris management and operation.
1979, 17 Oct Ran aground in the Aegean Sea during cruise. Heavily damaged; refloated and later repaired.

Santa Maria made worldwide headline news during the terrorist hijacking in January 1961 (*Alex Duncan*)

Companhia Colonial

SANTA MARIA

Service Lisbon, Vigo, Funchal and Tenerife to Port Everglades, Florida. Occasional stopovers in the Caribbean at San Juan, La Guaira and Curaçao.
Particulars 20,906 tons gross; 609x76x27ft.
Builders Cockerill-Ougree Shipyard at Hoboken, Belgium, 1953.
Machinery Steam turbines geared to twin screw; service speed 20 knots.
Capacity 156 first class, 226 cabin class and 696 third class. Third class used only for passengers to the Caribbean ports.
Notes The only major passenger liner to be hijacked by terrorists.

1952, 20 Sept Launched.
1953 Sept Maiden sailing from Lisbon to South America; also sailings from Lisbon to the Caribbean.
1956 Commenced service Lisbon-Caribbean-Florida.
1961, 22 Jan Hijacked in the Caribbean by Portuguese political rebels; rerouted to Brazil.
1961, 2 Feb Arrived at Recife; passengers freed. Later, rebels surrendered and ship returned to her owners.
1973, 19 July Arrived at Kaohsiung, Taiwan, for scrapping.

Federico C. was the first liner to be built directly for Costa Line (*Michael Cassar*)

Costa Line

FEDERICO C.

Service 1966-70: Naples, Genoa, Cannes, Barcelona, Lisbon and Funchal to Port Everglades. Florida. Winter cruising.
Particulars 20,416 tons gross; 606x79x27ft.
Builders Ansaldo Shipyard, Genoa, Italy, 1958.
Machinery Steam turbines geared to twin screw; service speed 21 knots.
Capacity 243 first class, 300 cabin class and 736 tourist class.
Notes First passenger liner built directly for Costa Line.

1957, 31 Mar Launched.
1958,22 Mar Left Genoa on maiden voyage to Rio de Janeiro, Montevideo and Buenos Aires; thereafter Italy-South America service.
1966 Apr Commenced special new service Mediterranean-Florida.
1968 Accommodation restyled as 186 first class and 1,450 tourist class.
1970 Cruising only.
1973, 8 Dec Grounded at Port Everglades; later refloated.
1976-7 Given $2 million refit, upgrading accommodation.
1977 Winter cruising in the Caribbean from Port Everglades and summer in the Mediterranean from Genoa.

The long and slender *Aquitania* was the last liner to have four funnels (*Frank O. Braynard Collection*)

Cunard Line

AQUITANIA

Service Post-war austerity service Southampton-Halifax: 12 voyages in 1948, 13 in 1949.
Particulars 45,647 tons gross; 901x97x36ft.
Builders John Brown & Company Limited, Clydebank, Scotland, 1914.
Machinery Steam triple-expansion turbines geared to quadruple screw; service speed 23.5 knots.
Capacity Approximately 2,200 in a single austerity class.
Notes One of the world's great liners; the last four-stack passenger ship.

1910 Dec Designed to serve with the original *Mauretania* and *Lusitania*.
1913, 21 Apr Launched.
1914 May Sea trials.
1914 Aug Converted to an Armed Merchant Cruiser for war service.
1915 Used as a hospital ship.
1916-18 Used as a troopship.
1919 June Returned to Southampton-New York commercial service: 618 first, 614 second and 1,998 third-class passengers.
1919 Dec Converted from coal to oil fuel.
1939-48 British Government trooping.
1948-9 Canadian immigrant service Southampton-Halifax.
1949, 1 Dec Completed final voyage at Southampton: 443 sailings, 35 years of service, 3 million steaming miles and 1.2 million passengers.
1950 Scrapped at Faslane, Scotland.

A BBC-TV crew filmed the final arrival of *Scythia* at Inverkeithing on 1 January 1958. She had finished thirty-seven years of service (*J. K. Byass*)

SCYTHIA

Service 1950-7: most sailings between London or Southampton, Le Havre and Quebec City. occasional sailings to New York via Halifax.
Particulars 19,930 tons gross; 624x73ft.
Builders Vickers-Armstrong Shipbuilders Limited, Barrow-in-Furness, England, 1920.
Machinery Steam turbines geared to twin screw; service speed 16 knots.
Capacity 248 first class and 630 tourist class.

1920, 22 Mar Launched; completed at L'Orient, France, owing to British shipbuilding strikes.
1921, 20 Aug Maiden voyage from Liverpool to New York (350 first class, 350 second class and 1,500 third class).
1939-48 Government trooping service.
1942, 23 Nov Damaged in bombing at Algiers; towed to Gibraltar and then New York for repairs.
1948 Made ten round-trip voyages Cuxhaven (Hamburg)-Le Havre-Quebec City or Halifax.
1949 Nov Commenced major refit for restoration to peacetime service.
1950, 17 Aug Post-war maiden voyage from Liverpool to Quebec City; thereafter from Southampton or London via Le Havre.
1952, 5 June Collision in the St Lawrence River with the collier *Wabana*.
1957 Oct Final Cunard passenger-sailing Liverpool-Cobh-New York.
1957 Oct-Nov Two trooping voyages Quebec City-Rotterdam.
1957, 22 Dec Arrived at Southampton; laid-up.
1958, 1 Jan Sailed for Inverkeithing to be scrapped.

Samaria represented the Cunard Line at the Coronation Review at Spithead in June 1953 (*J. K. Byass*)

SAMARIA

Service 1950-7: most sailings between London or Southampton, Le Havre and Quebec City; winter sailings to Halifax.
Particulars 19,848 tons gross; 624x73ft.
Builders Cammell Laird & Company Limited, Birkenhead, England, 1921.
Machinery Steam turbines geared to twin screw; service speed 16 knots.
Capacity 250 first class and 650 tourist class.

1920, 27 Nov Launched.
1922, 19 Apr Maiden voyage from Liverpool to Boston (350 first class, 350 second class and 1,500 third class).
1926 Transferred to Liverpool-New York service, usually via Boston.
1939-48 Government trooping.
1948 Sept Hamburg-Le Havre-Quebec City or Halifax austerity service.
1950 London-Quebec City service.
1950 Oct Major refit; restored to commercial status; 250 first-class and 650 tourist-class passengers.
1951 June Commenced commercial sailings Southampton-Le Havre-Quebec City.
1953, 15 June Represented Cunard at the Coronation Review at Spithead.
1955 Nov Final Cunard sailing from Quebec City to Southampton.
1956 Jan Sold to scrappers at Inverkeithing.

Winston Churchill and his staff used *Franconia* as accommodation during the Yalta Conference in February 1945 (*F. W. Hawks*)

FRANCONIA

Service Post-war sailings between Liverpool and Quebec City, and between Liverpool, Cobh, Halifax and New York.
Particulars 20,341 tons gross; 623x73ft.
Builders John Brown & Company Limited, Clydebank, Scotland, 1923.
Machinery Steam turbines geared to twin screw; service speed 16 knots.
Capacity 250 first class and 600 tourist class.

1922, 21 Oct Launched.
1923, 23 June Maiden voyage from Liverpool to New York.
1929-39 Liverpool or London-New York service and much cruising.
1930-1 Major refit.
1939 Sept Commenced Government trooping.
1939, 5 Oct Collided with the Royal Mail Liner *Alcantara* in the Mediterranean; damage repaired.
1940, 16 June Damaged by bombers off France; repaired.
1945 Feb Used as Winston Churchill's floating headquarters and accommodation during the Yalta Conference.
1948-9 Major refit and restoration for peacetime service.
1949, 2 June Post-war maiden voyage from Liverpool to Quebec City.
1956 Nov Final Cunard sailing from New York to Liverpool.
1956 Dec Sailed from Liverpool to Inverkeithing for scrapping.

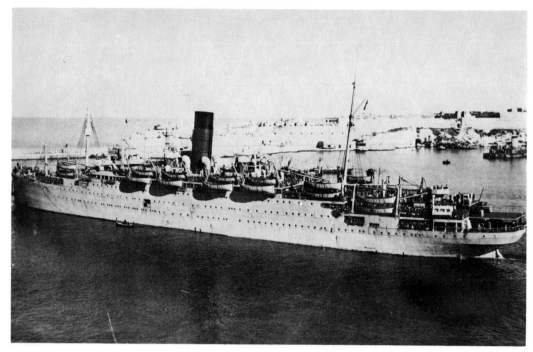

Ascania painted in grey during the war years (*Michael Cassar*)

ASCANIA

Service Liverpool to Quebec City and Montreal during the summer season; to Halifax during the winters.
Particulars 14,440 tons gross; 538x65ft.
Builders Armstrong-Whitworth Company Limited, Newcastle-upon-Tyne, England, 1925.
Machinery Steam turbines geared to twin screw; service speed 15 knots.
Capacity 198 first class and 498 tourist class.

1923, 20 Dec Launched.
1925, 22 May Maiden voyage from London and Southampton to Quebec City and Montreal: 500 cabin class and 1,200 third class; also cruising.
1938, 2 July Aground in the St Lawrence.
1939-48 Government trooping.
1949 Major refit for return to peacetime service.
1950, 21 Apr Maiden post-war sailing Liverpool-Quebec City-Montreal.
1956 Nov Final Cunard sailing Montreal-Southampton.
1956 Dec Trooping voyage to Port Said.
1956, 30 Dec Departed from Southampton for Newport, Monmouthshire, for scrapping.

Britannic's forward funnel was a dummy which housed wireless equipment (*Alex Duncan*)

BRITANNIC

Service Liverpool and Cobh to New York; annual winter cruise from New York to the Mediterranean and Black Sea.
Particulars 27,666 tons gross; 712x82ft.
Builders Harland & Wolff Limited, Belfast, Northern Ireland, 1930.
Machinery B&W-type diesels geared to twin screw; service speed 18 knots.
Capacity 429 first class and 564 tourist class.
Notes The last liner to wear the colours of the original White Star Line.

1929, 6 Aug Launched for White Star Line.
1930, 28 June Commenced maiden voyage from Liverpool to New York: 504 cabin-class, 551 tourist-class and 498 third-class passengers.
1934 Acquired as part of the Cunard-White Star merger.
1935 Transferred to the London-Le Havre-Southampton-New York service.
1939-47 Government trooping.
1947-8 Major refit for commercial service: tonnage revised from 26,943 to 27,666; capacity reduced to 993 passenger berths.
1948, 22 May Maiden post-war sailing from Liverpool to New York via Cobh.
1960 June Broken crankshaft; idle at New York.
1960 Dec Sold for scrap at Inverkeithing.

Georgic was drastically rebuilt after the war with a single funnel and mast (*Real Photographs Limited*)

GEORGIC

Service Post-war Cunard charter sailings between Liverpool or Southampton, Le Havre and Cobh to Halifax and New York during the summers; winter immigrant service to Australia.
Particulars 27,469 tons gross; 711x82ft.
Builders Harland & Wolff Limited, Belfast, Northern Ireland, 1932.
Machinery B&W-type diesels geared to twin screw; service speed 18 knots.
Capacity 1,962 one-class passengers.
Notes The last liner built for the original White Star Line.

1931, 12 Nov Launched.
1932 June Completed; entered Liverpool-New York service.
1934 Acquired in Cunard-White Star merger.
1935 Transferred to London-Le Havre-Southampton-New York service.
1939 Became troopship for war duties.
1941, 14 Sept Bombed and set afire at Port Tewfik, Egypt.
1941, 27 Oct Salvaged.
1941, 29 Dec Commenced tow to Port Sudan.
1942, 31 Mar Reached Karachi.
1942 Dec At Bombay; further repairs.
1943 Jan Bombay to Liverpool; major rebuilding at Belfast. Sold to the Ministry of Transport; forward funnel removed.
1944 Dec Finally returned to service.
1948 Converted to one-class immigrant ship.
1949 Jan Commenced Liverpool-Sydney service.
1950-4 Chartered to Cunard for summer-season Atlantic sailings.
1954 Oct Final Cunard sailing New York-Halifax-Southampton.
1955 Final season on Australian immigrant service.
1956 Feb Scrapped at Faslane.

QUEEN MARY

Service Southampton, Cherbourg to New York.
Particulars 81,237 tons gross; 1,019x119x39ft.
Builders John Brown & Company Limited, Clydebank, Scotland, 1936.
Machinery Steam turbines geared to quadruple screw; service speed 28½ knots.
Capacity 711 first class, 707 cabin class and 577 tourist class.
Notes World's fastest liner from 1938 until 1952. First major Cunarder to dispense with the traditional 'ia' name ending; last three-funnel passenger liner.

1930, 27 Dec Keel laid.
1931 Dec-1934 Apr Construction halted owing to the Depression.
1934, 26 Sept Launched and named by Her Majesty Queen Mary.
1936, 27 May Commenced maiden voyage from Southampton to New York.
1936 Aug Captured Blue Riband from French *Normandie*, averaging over 30 knots.
1937 Mar Riband recaptured by *Normandie* at 30.9 knots.
1938 Aug Firmly retook Riband from *Normandie* at 31.6 knots; record stood until taken by *United States* in July 1952.
1939 Sept Laid-up at New York for safety.
1940, 1 Mar Commissioned as a troopship at New York.
1940, 5 May Sailed from Sydney as a troopship.
1942, 2 Oct Rammed and sank British cruiser *Curacoa* off Ireland; 338 casualties from the warship.
1946 Sept Decommissioned at Southampton; commenced major refit at Clydebank.
1947, 31 July Sailed from Southampton on first post-war voyage to New York.
1958 Stabilizers added during winter overhaul.
1963 Dec First cruise; Southampton to Las Palmas.
1967 Mar Rumour that Australian syndicate planned to buy ship for conversion to immigrant carrier.
1967 Loss of £750,000 in operations.
1967, 22 Sept Final sailing from New York.
1967 Oct Sold to the City of Long Beach, California for over $3 million.
1967, 31 Oct Left Southampton for last time, bound for farewell cruise around South America to Long Beach. Extensive refit at Long Beach Naval Shipyard costing over $40 million.
1971, 28 Feb Moved to permanent berth at Long Beach.
1971, 8 May Opened to the public as a museum, convention centre and hotel. Total renovations costing in excess of $60 million.
1978 Dec Rumoured to be for sale.
1980 Nov Management taken over by Wrather Corporation; to remain at Long Beach as hotel-museum-convention centre.

The illustrious *Queen Mary* — the last of the Atlantic three-stackers — at Southampton (*BCM Pictures*)

As a hotel and museum complex, the great *Queen* is permanently moored at Long Beach, California (*Queen Mary Hyatt Hotel*)

Stratheden was the first P&O liner to visit New York in peacetime (*Alex Duncan*)

STRATHEDEN

Service Cunard charter for four sailings between Southampton and New York in 1950.
Particulars 23,732 tons gross; 664x82x30ft.
Builders Vickers-Armstrong Shipbuilders Limited, Barrow-in-Furness, England, 1937.
Machinery Steam turbines geared to twin screw; service speed 19 knots.
Capacity 527 first class and 453 tourist class.
Notes First P&O liner to visit New York in peacetime.

1937, 10 June Launched by Duchess of Buccleuch and Queensferry.
1937 Dec Maiden voyage from London to Australia via Suez; P&O Lines flagship.
1938-9 Australian service and 14-day Mediterranean cruises from London.
1938-46 Government troopship service.
1946-7 Major refit for return to commercial service.
1947 June First post-war sailing to Australia.
1950 Four Cunard charter voyages between Southampton and New York.
1961 Accommodation restyled for 1,200 one-class passengers.
1964 Sold to John S. Latsis Line, Greek flag; renamed *Henrietta Latsi*. Used as a pilgrim ship in Mediterranean, African and Middle Eastern waters.
1966 Renamed *Marianna Latsi*.
1969, 19 May Arrived at La Spezia, Italy, for scrapping.

MAURETANIA

Service Southampton, Le Havre and Cobh to New York; winter cruising from New York to the Caribbean.
Particulars 35,655 tons gross; 772x89x30ft.
Builders Cammell Laird & Company Limited, Birkenhead, England, 1939.
Machinery Steam turbines geared to twin screw; service speed 23 knots.
Capacity 470 first class, 370 cabin class and 300 tourist class.

1938, 28 July Launched.
1939, 17 June Commenced maiden voyage from Liverpool to New York; thence on Southampton-Le Havre-New York sailings.
1939 Dec Laid-up at New York for safety.
1940, 6 Mar Sailed for Sydney and there converted for trooping.
1940-6 Government trooping.
1944, 8 Jan Collided with tanker *Hat Creek* outside New York.
1946, 2 Sept Decommissioned from war duties; refitted at Liverpool.
1947, 10 June First post-war sailing from Southampton to New York.
1957 Made fully air-conditioned.
1962 Dec Repainted in green and used mostly for cruising.
1963 Experimental season on the Naples-Genoa-Cannes-Gibraltar-New York run; unsuccessful. Further cruising.
1964 Oct Chartered to Regent Refining Company Limited to carry guests to opening of new refinery at Milford Haven.
1965, 23 Nov Arrived in Firth of Forth for scrapping; broken-up at Inverkeithing.

Mauretania in the traditional black hull and white superstructure colouring of the Cunard Line (*Alex Duncan*)

In 1962 she was repainted in green with an eye toward further cruising (*Cunard Line*)

QUEEN ELIZABETH

Service Southampton and Cherbourg to New York.
Particulars 83,673 tons gross; 1,031x119x39ft.
Builders John Brown & Company Limited, Clydebank, Scotland, 1940.
Machinery Steam turbines geared to twin screw; service speed 28½ knots.
Capacity 823 first class, 662 cabin class and 798 tourist class.
Notes The largest passenger liner ever built.

1936 Dec Keel laid.
1938, 27 Sept Launched by Her Majesty Queen Elizabeth (later Her Majesty the Queen Mother).
1940, 26 Feb Darted for safety direct from Clydebank to New York, arriving on 7 March.
1940 Nov Sailed from New York to Singapore.
1940-6 Wartime trooping: total of 800,000 passengers carried, 500,000 miles steamed.
1946, 6 Mar First Cunarder released from war service.
1946, 8 Mar Fire at Southampton; major refit.
1946, 16 Oct Maiden commercial voyage Southampton-New York.
1947 Aground at Bramble Bank for 24 hours.
1952, 4 Dec Collided with tug in New York harbour; slight damage.
1954 Carried Her Majesty Queen Elizabeth the Queen Mother as a passenger.
1954-5 During annual winter overhaul, fitted with stabilizers.
1959 Aug Collision outside New York harbour with United States Lines freighter *American Hunter.*
1960 Dec Refit.
1965 Dec Began three-month £1.5 million refit in Firth of Forth Graving Dock. Full air-conditioning and lido deck installed. Improvements to passenger and crew accommodation to ensure operation through to 1975. Tonnage revised to 82,998.
1967 Loss of £750,000 in operations.
1968, 8 Nov Final Cunard sailing: Southampton-Las Palmas-Gibraltar-Southampton cruise. Completed record of 907 Atlantic crossings, 3,470,000 miles and 2,300,000 passengers.
1968 Nov Sold to American financial interests.
1968, 29 Nov Departed from Southampton for Port Everglades, arriving there on December 8. Laid-up at Port Everglades; legal problems and bankruptcy.
1969, 19 July Sold to The Queen Limited, an American consortium, for £3.5 million. Remained idle at Port Everglades.
1970 July Bankrupt again.
1970, 9-10 Sept Auctioned-off for $3.2 million to Seawise Foundations Limited (C.Y.Tung Group), the Bahamas; renamed *Seawise University.*
1971, 10 Feb Departed from Port Everglades for Hong Kong via Capetown.
1971 Refitted as a floating university-cruiseship.
1972, 8-9 Jan Destroyed by fire at Hong Kong; capsized.
1972, 13 Jan Last fire extinguished. Talk of salvage by Smit-Tak International Salvage Company; later scrapped on the spot.

The magnificent *Queen Elizabeth*, one of the finest-looking passenger liners ever built (*Cunard Line*)

The great ship burning to death at Hong Kong on 8 January 1972 (*South China Morning Post Limited*)

MEDIA

Service Liverpool to New York; occasionally via Bermuda.
Particulars 13,345 tons gross; 531x70x30ft.
Builders John Brown & Company Limited, Clydebank, Scotland, 1947.
Machinery Steam turbines geared to twin screw; service speed 18 knots.
Capacity 250 first-class passengers.
Notes First post-war transatlantic liner to be completed; first Atlantic passenger liner to have fin stabilizers fitted.

1946, 12 Dec Launched.
1947 Aug Maiden voyage Liverpool-New York
1953 Jan During winter overhaul fitted with fin stabilizers.
1961 Sold to Cogedar Line, Italian flag; renamed *Flavia*. Thoroughly rebuilt at Genoa for immigrant trade with 1,320 berths; lengthened to 557ft.
1962 Dec First Australian sailing from Bremerhaven, Rotterdam, Southampton and Genoa.
1968 Transferred to Costa Line. Refitted: 800 one-class cruise passengers.
1968, 21 Dec First sailing on Miami-Nassau service.
1977 Returned to Mediterranean cruise service.
1978 Dec Transferred back to Miami-Nassau run.

PARTHIA

Service Liverpool to New York; occasionally via Bermuda.
Particulars 13,362 tons gross; 531x70x30ft.
Builders Harland & Wolff Limited, Belfast, Northern Ireland, 1948.
Machinery Steam turbines geared to twin screw; service speed 18 knots.
Capacity 250 first-class passengers.

1947, 25 Feb Launched.
1948, 10 Apr Began maiden voyage from Liverpool to New York.
1961 Nov Sold to New Zealand Shipping Company; renamed *Remuera* (qv).

Cunard's combination passenger-cargo ship *Media* was the first Atlantic passenger vessel to be fitted with fin stabilizers (*J. K. Byass*)

Media was totally rebuilt in 1961-2 as the Italian-flag *Flavia* (*Costa Line*)

CARONIA

Service Occasional Southampton-Le Havre-New York sailings. Mostly cruising: around-the-world or Pacific in January; Mediterranean in May; North Cape in June; Mediterranean in September. All sailings from New York with some terminating at Southampton.
Particulars 34,172 tons gross; 715x91x31ft.
Builders John Brown & Company Limited, Clydebank, Scotland, 1948.
Machinery Steam turbines geared to twin screw; service speed 22 knots.
Capacity 581 first class and 351 cabin class; 600 one-class for cruising.
Notes In 1949, the largest liner yet built with cruising in mind; also the largest single-funnel liner in the world.

1947, 30 Oct Launched and named by Her Royal Highness Princess Elizabeth (later Her Majesty Queen Elizabeth II).
1949, 4 Jan Left Southampton on maiden voyage to New York, then commenced cruising.
1958, 14 Apr Rammed a lighthouse at Yokohama, pushing it into the sea. Ship damaged; repaired at Yokohama.
1965 Oct Began three-month refit at Harland & Wolff yard, Belfast.
1967 Nov Laid-up.
1968 Jan Intended sale to Dumas Turist, Yugoslavia, for use as a floating hotel on the Dalmatian Coast never materialized.
1968, 24 May Sold to Star Line, Panama, for £1.2 million. Owners later retitled as Universal Line S/A, Panama. Renamed *Columbia*, then *Caribia*.
1968, 26 July Officially transferred to new owners.
1968 Sept Commenced refit at Piraeus, then at Naples.
1969, 14 Feb Maiden Caribbean cruise from New York as *Caribia*.
1969, 5 Mar Engine-room explosion in the Caribbean; towed to New York.
1969, 25 Mar Laid-up at New York.
1974, 27 Apr Left New York under tow for Taiwan for scrapping.
1974, 11 July At Honolulu with flooding problems.
1974, 12 Aug Put into Guam in heavy weather. Ship struck breakwater and broke in three sections; later dismantled on the spot.

The outbound *Caronia* during the 1950s (*Roger Scozzafava*)

Renamed *Caribia*, she was lashed by a tropical storm and wrecked at Guam in August 1974 (*United States Coast Guard*)

SAXONIA/CARMANIA

Service Southampton and Le Havre to Quebec City and Montreal during the summer, ice-free months; occasionally via Cobh. Winter sailings between London or Southampton, Le Havre, Halifax and New York.
Particulars 21,367 tons gross; 608x80x28ft.
Builders John Brown & Company Limited, Clydebank, Scotland, 1954.
Machinery Steam turbines geared to twin screw; service speed 19½ knots.
Capacity 125 first class and 800 tourist class.

1954, 17 Feb Launched as *Saxonia* by Lady Churchill.
1954, 2 Sept Left Liverpool on maiden voyage to Montreal; later switched to Southampton service.
1962-3 Major refit at Clydebank: repainted in green; air conditioning, lido deck and new public rooms added; accommodation restyled as 117 first class and 764 tourist class; renamed *Carmania*.
1963 Apr Commenced new Rotterdam-Southampton-Montreal summer service with winter Caribbean cruising from Port Everglades.
1967 Feb Hull repainted in white.
1969, 12 Jan Aground on San Salvador Island, the Bahamas; passengers taken ashore. Refloated on 17 January and ship sailed to Newport News, Virginia, for repairs.
1969, 14 May Collided with Soviet tanker *Frunze* off Gibraltar.
1971 Apr Reported discussions on sale to Chandris Group, Greek Flag; sale never materialized.
1971 Dec Laid-up.
1972, 15 May Transferred to River Fal for continued lay-up.
1972 May Proposed sale to Toyo Yusen K.K., Japan, for Far East cruising, never materialized.
1973 Aug Sold to Nikreis Maritime Corporation, as agents for the Black Sea Steamship Company, Odessa; renamed *Leonid Sobinov*, Soviet flag. Chartered to CTC Lines, London, for cruising and Southampton-Australia sailings.
1974, 25 Feb First Southampton-Sydney sailing.
1980 June Being used by the Cuban Government to transport troops from Havana to the Middle East and East Africa via Suez.

Saxonia was the first of four sisterships built for Cunard's Canadian service (*F. R. Sherlock*)

After being sold to the Soviets she began Australian and cruise service as *Leonid Sobinov* in 1974 (*Alex Duncan*)

IVERNIA/FRANCONIA

Service Southampton and Le Havre to Quebec City and Montreal during the summer, ice-free months; occasionally via Cobh. Winter sailings between London or Southampton, Le Havre, Halifax and New York.
Particulars 21,717 tons gross; 608x80x28ft.
Builders John Brown & Company Limited, Clydebank, Scotland, 1955.
Machinery Steam turbines geared to twin screw; service speed 19½ knots.
Capacity 125 first class and 800 tourist class.

1954, 14 Dec Launched.
1955, 1 July Maiden voyage Greenock-Quebec City-Montreal; thereafter based at Southampton.
1962-3 Major refit at Clydebank: repainted in green; air-conditioning, lido deck and new public rooms installed; accommodation revised as 119 first class and 728 tourist class; renamed *Franconia*; tonnage listed as 22,637.
1963 July Entered new Rotterdam-Southampton-Montreal service during the summers, with winter cruising from New York to the Caribbean.
1967 Feb Hull repainted in white.
1967 Apr Began weekly 7-day New York-Bermuda cruise service; longer Caribbean cruises during the winter season.
1970 Dec Engine trouble in the Caribbean; returned to Port Everglades.
1971 Apr Reported discussions with the Greek Chandris Group for possible purchase; later collapsed.
1971 Dec Laid-up.
1972 Jan Intended sale to Toyo Yusen K.K., Japan, never materialized.
1972, 15 May Transferred to River Fal for further lay-up.
1973 Aug Sold to Nikreis Maritime Corporation as agents for the Black Sea Steamship Company, Odessa; renamed *Feodor Shalyapin*, Soviet flag. Commenced refit.
1973, 20 Nov First sailing Southampton-Australian ports under charter to CTC Lines, London.
1980 June Being used by the Cuban Government to transport troops from Havana to the Middle East and East Africa via Suez.

Ivernia as she appeared at the time of her completion in June 1955 (*Alex Duncan*)

For cruising purposes she was refitted and painted in green as *Franconia* in 1963 (*Cunard Line*)

The superstructure and upperworks of *Carinthia* were completely rebuilt in 1970-1 when she became the cruiseship *Fairsea* (*Michael D. J. Lennon*)

CARINTHIA

Service Liverpool and Greenock to Quebec City and Montreal during the summer months; Liverpool and Cobh to Halifax and New York during the winter.
Particulars 21,947 tons gross; 608x80x28ft.
Builders John Brown & Company Limited, Clydebank, Scotland, 1956.
Machinery Steam turbines geared to twin screw; service speed 19½ knots.
Capacity 154 first class and 714 tourist class.

1954, 23 Dec Laid down.
1955, 14 Dec Launched and named by Her Royal Highness Princess Margaret.
1956, 27 June Maiden voyage from Liverpool to Quebec City and Montreal.
1967 Feb Hull repainted in white for winter cruising.
1967, 13 Oct Sailed from Liverpool on final Cunard passenger voyage to Quebec City and Montreal; later laid-up at Southampton.
1968, 4 May Sold to Sitmar Line, Liberian flag; renamed *Fairland*, then *Fairsea*. Continued in lay-up at Southampton.
1970, 21 Feb Arrived at Trieste for major rebuilding: 910 one-class passengers; tonnage revised to 21,916.
1971, 17 Dec Entered cruise service from San Francisco and Los Angeles to Mexico (summers to Alaska via Vancouver).
1976 Sept Damaged while in drydock at Alameda, California. Still in service.

Sylvania was repainted with a white hull in 1966 for increased use as a cruiseship (*Alex Duncan*)

SYLVANIA

Service Liverpool and Greenock to Quebec City and Montreal during the summer months; Liverpool and Cobh to Halifax and New York during the winter.
Particulars 21,989 tons gross; 608x80x28ft.
Builders John Brown & Company Limited, Clydebank, Scotland, 1957.
Machinery Steam turbines geared to twin screw; service speed 19½ knots.
Capacity 154 first class and 724 tourist class.

1956, 22 Nov Launched.
1957, 5 June Maiden voyage Liverpool-Quebec City-Montreal.
1961 Apr Transferred to year-round Liverpool-Cobh-New York service.
1964 Sept Refitted.
1964 Oct 27-day cruise to the Mediterranean, first such Cunard sailing from Liverpool since 1939.
1966, 24 Nov End of Cunard's Liverpool-New York service.
1966 Dec Repainted with white hull for further cruise work.
1968 May Laid-up at Southampton.
1968, 5 July Sold to Sitmar Line, Liberian flag; renamed *Fairwind*. Continued in lay-up at Southampton.
1970, 6 Jan Left Southampton under tow for Trieste, arriving 14 January. Major refit.
1972, 1 July Entered cruise service from San Francisco and Los Angeles; later transferred to base at Port Everglades.
1975, 29 Nov Fire and engine-room damage in the Caribbean. Still in service.

Queen Elizabeth 2, the last of the great transatlantic superliners (*Cunard Line*)

QUEEN ELIZABETH 2

Service May-November sailings between Southampton, Cherbourg and New York; considerable cruising.
Particulars 65,863 tons gross; 963x105x32ft.
Builders Upper Clyde Shipbuilders Limited (formerly John Brown & Company Limited yards), Clydebank, Scotland, 1969.
Machinery Steam turbines geared to twin screw; service speed 28½ knots.
Capacity 564 first class and 1,441 tourist class; 1,400 one-class for cruising.
Notes Last great superliner to be built.

1965, 5 June Keel laid.
1967, 20 Sept Launched and named by Her Majesty Queen Elizabeth.
1968, 26 Nov Left Greenock for trials: serious turbine problems and other defects; Cunard refused delivery from the shipbuilder.
1969, 2 Jan Docked at Southampton for the first time; Cunard still refused acceptance.
1969 Mar Fresh trials, averaging 32.66 knots.
1969, 18 Apr Finally delivered to Cunard; delays cost £3 million.
1969, 2 May Left Southampton on maiden voyage to New York.
1971, 9 Jan Rescued survivors from the burning French liner *Antilles* off Mustique in the Caribbean.
1972 Capacity restyled as 604 first class and 1,223 tourist class with 1,740 one-class for cruising.
1974, 1 Apr Immobilized by boiler trouble, 280 miles southwest of Bermuda.
1974, 3 Apr 1,630 passengers transferred at sea to the nearby cruiseship *Sea Venture*.
1974, 7 Apr Towed to Bermuda.
1975 Dec Damaged hull on a coral reef at Nassau.
1976, 23 July Engine-room fire; forced to return to Southampton.
1976 Capacity listed as 1,820 one-class passengers for all sailings.
1977 Dec New suites added and ship remeasured as 67,107 tons gross.
1978 Sept Damaged in North Atlantic storm.
1979 Dec Extensive refit at Bayonne, New Jersey.

Captain Cook, as she appeared after the war (*Alex Duncan*)

Donaldson Line

CAPTAIN COOK

Service Seven charter sailings in 1955: Glasgow-Liverpool-Quebec City-Montreal service.
Particulars 13,876 tons gross; 538x66ft.
Builders Fairfield Shipbuilding & Engineering Company, Glasgow, Scotland, 1925.
Machinery Steam turbines geared to twin screw; service speed 15 knots.
Capacity 1,088 one-class passengers.

1924, 14 Oct Launched as *Letitia* for Donaldson Line.
1925, 25 Apr Maiden voyage Glasgow-Quebec City-Montreal: 516 cabin class and 1,023 third class.
1933 Accommodation restyled as 298 cabin class, 310 tourist class and 964 third class.
1939-44 Government wartime trooping.
1944-6 Hospital ship.
1946 Sold to British Ministry of Transport but managed by Donaldson; renamed *Empire Brent*.
1947 Rebuilt as a peacetime troopship.
1948 India and Far East services.
1950 Glasgow-Sydney immigrant service.
1951-2 Refitted at Glasgow: 1,088 one-class passengers; renamed *Captain Cook*; restyled as an Australian immigrant ship.
1955 Chartered to Donaldson for seven sailings to Canada.
1956-60 Australian service.
1960, 29 Apr Arrived at Inverkeithing for scrapping.

Lismoria was rebuilt for passenger service from a standard wartime 'Victory' class freighter (*Donaldson Line*)

LISMORIA

Service Glasgow direct to Montreal. Until 1955, winter service to North American Pacific Coast ports via Panama Canal; after 1955, winter sailings to Saint John, NB, and Halifax.
Particulars 8,323 tons gross; 455x62x28ft.
Builders California Shipbuilding Corporation, Los Angeles, California, 1945.
Machinery Steam turbines geared to single screw; service speed 15 knots.
Capacity 55 first-class passengers.
Notes Former freighter rebuilt as a passenger-cargo liner.

1945, 31 Jan Delivered to War Shipping Administration, American flag, as the 'Victory' class freighter-transport *Taos Victory*.
1946 Transferred to the British Ministry of War Transport; managed by Furness Withy & Company. Refitted as a freighter.
1948 Sold to Donaldson Line. Rebuilt with 55 passenger berths; intended to be renamed *Cabotia* but named *Lismoria* instead.
1948, 10 Oct Maiden sailing from Glasgow to Montreal.
1966 Withdrawn, thus ending Donaldson passenger services.
1966 Nov Sold to Astroguarda Cia Navigation S/A, Greek flag; renamed *Neon*. Used as a freighter.
1967 May Scrapped at Kaohsiung, Taiwan.

Laurentia was similarly fitted with fifty-five first-class berths (*Alex Duncan*)

LAURENTIA

Service Glasgow direct to Montreal. Until 1955, winter service to North American Pacific Coast ports via Panama Canal; after 1955, winter sailings to Saint John, NB, and Halifax.
Particulars 8,349 tons gross; 455x62x28ft.
Builders Permanent Shipyard No 1, Richmond, California, 1945.
Machinery Steam turbines geared to single screw; service speed 15 knots.
Capacity 55 first-class passengers.
Notes Former freighter rebuilt as a passenger-cargo liner. As built, she was the first American merchant ship to be fitted with radar.

1945 Mar Delivered to the War Shipping Administration, American flag, as the 'Victory' class freighter-transport *Medina Victory*.
1946 June Transferred to the British Ministry of War Transport; managed by Donaldson Line.
1947 Sept Commenced refit at Barclay Curle Shipyard, Glasgow; renamed *Laurentia*.
1949 Rebuilt with 55 passenger berths.
1949, 12 May Departed from Glasgow on maiden voyage to Montreal.
1966 Withdrawn, thus ending Donaldson passenger services.
1967, 4 Jan Arrived at Valencia, Spain, for scrapping.

Royal Rotterdam Lloyd's *Sibajak* was primarily used on the Indonesian passenger run but made periodic transatlantic voyages with immigrants and students (*Herbert G. Frank, Jr*)

Dutch World Services

SIBAJAK

Service Occasional summer sailings between Rotterdam, Halifax and New York; also some sailings to Quebec City.
Particulars 12,342 tons gross; 530x62ft.
Builders De Schelde Shipyards, Flushing, Holland, 1928.
Machinery Sulzer diesels geared to twin screw; service speed 17 knots.
Capacity 1,000 one-class passengers.

1927, 2 Apr Launched. Owned by Royal Rotterdam Lloyd.
1928, 8 Feb Maiden voyage from Rotterdam to the East Indies: 527 passengers in three classes.
1935 Major refit: tonnage revised to 12,226.
1940-8 Wartime trooping under P&O Lines management.
1949 Refitted as immigrant ship with 1,000 berths.
1950 Rotterdam-Sydney immigrant service.
1951 Rotterdam-Indonesia service.
1952 Apr Began sailings between Rotterdam and Quebec City.
1954, 5 May Rotterdam-Halifax-New York sailings.
1955 Rotterdam-Indonesia service.
1959, 25 Aug Arrived at Hong Kong for scrapping.

Nederland Line's *Johan van Oldenbarnevelt* as built in 1930 with squat funnels and numerous deck cargo cranes (*Alex Duncan*)

Following her 1958-9 refit, the ship was fitted with new domed funnels and repainted with a dove-grey hull (*Nederland Line*)

JOHAN VAN OLDENBARNEVELT

Service Occasional student voyages between Amsterdam or Rotterdam, Southampton and New York. Between 1959 and 1962, eastbound sailings from Port Everglades and occasionally New York to Southampton and Amsterdam.
Particulars 19,787 tons gross; 608x74x27ft.
Builders Netherlands Shipbuilding Company, Amsterdam, Holland, 1930.
Machinery Sulzer diesels geared to twin screw; service speed 17 knots.
Capacity 1951-9: 1,414 one-class passengers. 1959-63: 1,186 one-class passengers.

1929, 3 Aug Launched, at the time the largest ship ever built in Holland. Owned by Nederland Line.
1930 May Maiden voyage from Amsterdam to the East Indies via Suez.
1939 Sept Transatlantic crossing to New York for evacuation purposes on behalf of Holland-America Line.
1940 Refitted as a troopship at Belfast; continuous war service.
1945 Oct Final trooping voyage Bombay-Southampton.
1946 Special Dutch Government trooping service to Indonesia and immigrant sailings to Australia.
1951 Refitted at Amsterdam: given 1,414 one-class berths. Continued Australian immigrant sailings.
1954 June One Atlantic crossing with students Rotterdam-Quebec City.
1954-8 Occasional crossings to New York together with Australian sailings.
1958-9 Major refit at Amsterdam: greatly improved accommodation for 1,186 passengers; new funnels added and hull repainted in grey; tonnage relisted as 20,314.
1959 Apr Commenced new around-the-world service: Amsterdam-Southampton-Palma-Genoa-Port Said-Suez-Colombo-Fremantle-Melbourne-Sydney-Wellington-Auckland-Suva-Papeete-Callao-Cristobal-Port Everglades-New York-Southampton-Amsterdam.
1963 Sold to Shipping Investment Corporation/Greek Line (Goulandris Group), Greek flag; sale price $1.2 million. Renamed *Lakonia*; refitted for cruise service from Southampton to the Canary Islands and Mediterranean.
1963, 22 Dec During a Christmas cruise, destroyed by fire off Madeira; 128 passengers and crew perished.
1963, 29 Dec Capsized and sank 250 miles west of Gibraltar while empty and under tow.

ORANJE

Service Occasional westbound voyages from Amsterdam and Southampton to New York and mostly Port Everglades. Part of around-the-world service: Amsterdam-Southampton-New York (occasionally)-Port Everglades-Panama-Papeete-Auckland-Wellington-Sydney-Melbourne-Singapore-Penang-Colombo-Port Said-Genoa-Southampton-Amsterdam.
Particulars 20,551 tons gross; 656x83x28ft.
Builders Netherlands Shipbuilding Company, Amsterdam, Holland, 1939.
Machinery Sulzer diesels geared to triple screw; service speed 21.5 knots.
Capacity 323 first class and 626 tourist class.

1938, 8 Sept Launched by Her Majesty Queen Wilhelmina; owned by the Nederland Line.
1939 July Completed; world's fastest motorliner.
1939 Sept Maiden voyage from Amsterdam to the East Indies via Suez.
1939 Dec-1941 Feb Laid-up at Surabaya for safety.
1941 Feb Commenced five-month conversion to a hospital ship at Sydney.
1941-6 Hospital ship with Royal Australian Navy although remaining under the Dutch flag.
1946, 19 July Returned to Nederland Line. Refitted after war service: tonnage listed as 20,017.
1946-50 Amsterdam-East Indies sailings.
1950-8 Amsterdam-Australia sailings and around-the-world voyages.
1953 Collision with *Willem Ruys*.
1959 Thoroughly refitted at Amsterdam: passenger accommodation restyled to take 949 berths; tonnage revised as 20,551.
1959-64 Around-the-world sailings including calls at New York and Port Everglades.
1962 May Made special cruise into the North Sea with large contingent of royalty aboard for Her Majesty Queen Juliana's Silver Wedding celebrations.
1964 Sept Sold and transferred to Lauro Line, Italian flag; sale price £1.3 million.
1965 Renamed *Angelina Lauro*. Commenced major rebuilding at Genoa.
1965, 24 Aug Heavy fire damage at Genoa shipyards: 6 workmen killed.
1966, 6 Mar Maiden voyage from Bremerhaven and Southampton to Australia via Suez: 189 first-class and 1,427 tourist-class passengers; had been lengthened to 672ft and tonnage listed as 24,377.
1973 Permanently assigned to cruising; 800 one-class passengers.
1977, 21 Oct Commenced three-year charter to Costa Line; name modified to *Angelina*. Caribbean cruising from San Juan, Puerto Rico, and summer Mediterranean cruises from Genoa.
1979, 31 Mar Gutted by fire at St Thomas; total loss.
1979, 26 May Salvage commenced.
1979, 2 July First raised.
1979, 6 July Fully afloat.
1979, 30 July Left St Thomas under tow of Japanese tug *Nippon Maru*; bound for scrapping at Kaohsiung via Panama Canal.
1979, 24 Sept Sank while under tow in the Pacific.

When brand-new *Oranje* was the world's fastest motorliner (*F. R. Sherlock*)

As *Angelina Lauro* she was totally rebuilt; note the new winged, smoke-deflecting funnel (*Alex Duncan*)

WILLEM RUYS

Service Around-the-world sailings that included eastbound sailings from Port Everglades, Bermuda and occasionally New York to Southampton and Rotterdam. Full itinerary: Rotterdam-Southampton-Port Said-Suez-Colombo-Singapore-Melbourne-Sydney-Wellington-Callao (occasionally)-Balboa-Cristobal-Miami-Bermuda-New York-Southampton-Rotterdam.
Particulars 23,114 tons gross; 631x82x29ft.
Builders De Schelde Shipyard, Flushing, Holland, 1947.
Machinery Sulzer diesels geared to twin screw; service speed 22 knots.
Capacity 275 first class and 770 tourist class.

1939 Laid down.
1939-45 Sluggish work effort owing to the war.
1946 Construction work accelerated; launched.
1947 Nov Trials, averaging 24.6 knots.
1947, 21 Nov Her owners, Rotterdam Lloyd, given 'royal' prefix by Her Majesty Queen Wilhelmina, becoming Royal Rotterdam Lloyd.
1947 Dec Entered service: Rotterdam-Southampton-Mediterranean-Suez-Aden-Indonesia.
1953 Collided with *Oranje*; damaged.
1958 First sailing to New York; also two charter sailings to Montreal from Rotterdam for Europe-Canada Line.
1958, 20 Sept-1959, 25 Feb Major refit at Schiedam: passenger accommodation modernized; funnels raised in height; tonnage increased from 21,119 to 23,114.
1959 Mar Entered new around-the-world service.
1964 Dec Sold and transferred to Lauro Line, Italian flag, for £3.4 million.
1965 Renamed *Achille Lauro*; commenced extensive refit at Palermo.
1965, 29 Aug Badly damaged by fire at Palermo shipyards.
1966, 7 Apr Extensively modernized with new fin funnels; tonnage listed as 23,629; 152 first-class and approximately 1,500 tourist-class passengers.
1972, 19 May Heavy damage by fire at Genoa; later repaired.
1972 Dec Permanent cruise service from Genoa.
1975, 28 Apr Collided with and sank the 497-ton Lebanese freighter *Youssef* off the Turkish coast.

Willem Ruys passing through the Panama Canal in 1959 (*Royal Rotterdam Lloyd*)

She was thoroughly modernized when she became *Achille Lauro* in 1965 (*Alex Duncan*)

The almost eccentric-looking *Erria*, without a conventional funnel and where exhausts were worked through the third mast (*East Asiatic Company*)

East Asiatic Company

ERRIA

Service Copenhagen-New York service 1949-51.
Particulars 7,670 tons gross; 463x62x25ft.
Builders Nakskov Skibsvaerft, Nakskov, Denmark, 1932.
Machinery B&W-type diesels geared to twin screw; service speed 16 knots.
Capacity 74 first-class passengers.
Notes 'Funnel-less' ship; exhausts were worked through the mast.

1934-9 Copenhagen-Far East via Suez service.
1940-5 Laid-up during the war.
1946-9 Copenhagen-Far East service.
1949-51 Copenhagen-New York service.
1950, 21 Oct Rammed by freighter *Pelican State* near New York harbour, south of Ambrose Light; damage; repaired.
1951 Dec Badly damaged by fire while sailing off Portland, Oregon, during a voyage from Copenhagen to the North American Pacific coast.
1952-62 Copenhagen-Far East service and worldwide freighter service.
1962 Scrapped at Osaka, Japan.

Jutlandia was the largest of East Asiatic's 'funnel-less' fleet. Notice the Maierform bow, which tended to increase speed and was used on a number of European combination ships (*East Asiatic Company*)

JUTLANDIA

Service Copenhagen-New York 1946-50.
Particulars 8,542 tons gross; 460x61x25ft.
Builders Nakskov Skibsvaerft, Nakskov, Denmark, 1934.
Machinery B&W-type diesels geared to twin screw; service speed 14 knots.
Capacity 69 first-class passengers.
Notes 'Funnel-less' ship; exhausts were worked through the mast.

1934-9 Copenhagen-Far East service.
1939-46 Laid-up.
1946 Mar Commenced Copenhagen-New York sailings.
1950 Withdrawn from transatlantic service and converted into a hospital ship for the Korean War.
1954 Rebuilt and returned to commercial service.
1954-64 Copenhagen-Far East service.
1965, 9 Jan Arrived at Bilbao, Spain, for scrapping.

The exhaust pipes on the third of *Falstria*'s four masts are clearly evident in this photograph (*East Asiatic Company*)

FALSTRIA

Service Copenhagen-New York service during 1952.
Particulars 6,993 tons gross; 453x63x25ft.
Builders Nakskov Skibsvaerft, Nakskov, Denmark, 1941-5.
Machinery B&W-type diesels geared to single screw; service speed 15 knots.
Capacity 54 first-class passengers.
Notes Funnel-less ship; exhausts were worked through the mast.

1941 Launched, then laid-up.
1945 May Damaged during the Allied air attacks on Nakskov.
1945 Nov Completed; entered Copenhagen-Far East service.
1952 Copenhagen-New York service.
1953 Returned to Copenhagen-Far East service.
1964 Sold to Greek buyers and renamed *Veryr*, then resold to Japanese shipbreakers.

Seven Seas as she appeared when first refitted for Europe-Canada Line in 1955 (*Holland-America Line*)

The funnel was later heightened as shown in this view from the 1960s (*Alex Duncan*)

Europe-Canada Line

SEVEN SEAS

Service Bremerhaven and/or Rotterdam, Le Havre, Southampton to Quebec City and Montreal or New York; occasional calls at Halifax. Winter: around-the-world cruises as a floating university.
Particulars 12,575 tons gross; 492x69x22ft.
Builders Sun Shipbuilding & Drydock Company, Chester, Pennsylvania, 1940.
Machinery Sulzer diesels geared to single screw; service speed 16.5 knots.
Capacity 20 first-class and 987 tourist-class passengers.
Notes Former freighter and aircraft carrier rebuilt as a passenger ship.

1940 Completed as *Mormacmail*, C3-type freighter, for Moore McCormack Lines, American flag.
1941, 6 Mar Transferred to the United States Navy and rebuilt as an auxiliary aircraft carrier.
1941, 2 June Commissioned as the USS *Long Island*.
1941-6 Military service.
1946 Apr Decommissioned; laid-up.
1948 Mar Sold to the Caribbean Land & Shipping Company, Panamanian flag. Rebuilt as an immigrant ship; renamed *Nelly*.
1949-55 Europe-Australia immigrant sailings.
1955 Apr Acquired by Europe-Canada Line (Caribbean Land & Shipping Corporation, Geneva), a creation of Holland-America Line and Royal Rotterdam Lloyd; renamed *Seven Seas*, Panamanian flag.
1955, 30 Apr Maiden sailing from Bremerhaven to Le Havre, Southampton, Quebec City and Montreal.
1955 July Transferred to West German flag; rumour that ship was to be renamed *Bremen* never materialized.
1965, 18 July Immobilized in North Atlantic by engine-room fire; repairs lasted until June 1966.
1966, 24 Sept Became hostel at Rotterdam for foreign workers of Verolme Shipyards; permanently moored.
1977, 4 May Left Rotterdam under tow; scrapped at Ghent, Belgium.

French Line

DE GRASSE

Service Le Havre, Southampton (or Plymouth) to New York 1947-51.
Particulars 18,435 tons gross; 574x71x29ft.
Builders Cammell Laird & Company, Birkenhead, England, 1924.
Machinery Steam turbines geared to twin screw; service speed 16 knots.
Capacity 500 first class and 470 tourist class.

1918 Laid down as *Suffren* for French Line: construction halted until 1923.
1924, 23 Feb Launched as *De Grasse*.
1924, 21 Aug Maiden voyage from Le Havre to New York: 17,707 tons gross; 536 cabin-class and 410 third-class passengers.
1940 Seized by the Nazi forces and used as an accommodation ship in the River Gironde near Bordeaux.
1944, 30 Aug Scuttled by retreating Nazi army at Bordeaux.
1945, 30 Aug Salvaged; sent to St Nazaire and rebuilt with one funnel. Tonnage listed as 18,435; 970 passengers.
1947, 12 July Reopened French Line's transatlantic service, Le Havre-New York.
1951, 30 Sept Last sailing from New York to Le Havre.
1952 Apr Assigned to Le Havre-West Indies service.
1953, 26 Mar Sold to Canadian Pacific Steamships Limited, British flag, renamed *Empress of Australia* (qv).

De Grasse as she appeared in 1924 with two thin funnels (*Frank O. Braynard Collection*)

Following her 1945-7 refit she was modernized and fitted with a single wide funnel (*French Line*)

ILE DE FRANCE

Service Le Havre, Southampton (or Plymouth) and New York. Winter cruising to the Caribbean.
Particulars 44,356 tons gross; 792x91ft.
Builders Chantiers de l'Atlantique, St Nazaire, France, 1927.
Machinery Steam turbines geared to quadruple screw; service speed 23.5 knots.
Capacity 541 first class, 577 cabin class and 227 tourist class.
Notes One of the most illustrious and popular liners ever built.

1926, 14 Mar Launched.
1927, 22 June Departed from Le Havre on maiden voyage to New York: 43,153 tons gross; 670 first-class, 408 second-class and 508 third-class passengers.
1932 Nov-1933 Apr Major refit; attempts made to reduce great vibration.
1939 Sept Laid-up at New York for safety.
1940 Troopship service.
1940, 19 July Seized at Singapore by the British forces; managed by Cunard-White Star.
1945, 22 Sept Reverted to French flag under Cunard management.
1946, 22 Oct Began austerity sailings between Cherbourg and New York.
1947 Apr Commenced major refit at St Nazaire: three funnels reduced to two, tonnage revised to 44,356; passenger accommodation restyled as 541 first class, 577 cabin class and 227 tourist class.
1949, 21 July Commercial post-war maiden voyage Le Havre-New York.
1956, 26 July Rescued 753 survivors from *Andrea Doria* – *Stockholm* collision off Nantucket.
1957 Feb Went aground on Martinique during a cruise. Damaged; towed to Newport News Shipyard in Virginia for repairs.
1958, 10 Nov Final transatlantic sailing New York-Plymouth-Le Havre.
1958 Dec Laid-up and offered for sale.
1959, 26 Feb Departed from Le Havre for Osaka as *Furansu Maru*, Japanese flag, for scrapping.
1959, 9 Apr Arrived at Osaka. Briefly used as a floating prop for film *The Last Voyage*.
1959 Sept Demolition completed.

Ile de France, with her original three funnels and painted in wartime grey while docked at a Weehawken, New Jersey, shipyard in 1945 (*Todd Shipyards Corporation*)

The illustrious *Ile* as she appeared after her 1947-9 refit with two wider funnels. Notice the ship s name in neon letters on the Sun Deck (*French Line*)

LIBERTE

Service Le Havre, Southampton (or Plymouth) to New York.
Particulars 51,839 tons gross; 936x102x34ft.
Builders Blohm & Voss A/G, Hamburg, Germany, 1930.
Machinery Steam turbines geared to quadruple screw; service speed 24 knots.
Capacity 555 first class, 497 cabin class and 450 tourist class.
Notes Briefly captured Blue Riband in 1930 as world's fastest liner; French flagship and largest liner 1946-61.

1928, 15 Aug Launched as *Europa* for North German Lloyd, German flag.
1929, 26 Mar Nearly destroyed in fire at shipyard; subsequently repaired: 49,746 tons gross; 2,024 passengers in four classes.
1930, 19 Mar Left Bremerhaven on maiden voyage to New York. Captured Blue Riband with average speed of 27.9 knots.
1939 Sept Laid-up at Bremerhaven. Fitted out for the intended Nazi invasion of Britain.
1945 May Seized by invading American forces at Bremerhaven; became troopship USS *Europa*. Plagued by small fires.
1946 June Awarded by United Nations Reparations Committee to France; transferred to French Line. Intended name *Lorraine* changed in favour of *Liberté*.
1946, 9 Dec Broke away from moorings at Le Havre during a storm; slammed against the sunken hull of the *Paris* and partially sank.
1947, 15 Apr Refloated; towed to St Nazaire for thorough refitting. Cost $19 million.
1950, 17 Aug Left Le Havre on maiden voyage to New York; tonnage listed as 51,839.
1954 Feb Funnels raised in height with new dome tops.
1961 Nov Final sailing from New York to Le Havre. Rumoured to become floating hotel at Seattle for 1962 World's Fair.
1961 Dec Sold to India Shipping & Trading Company, Vaduz, Liechtenstein.
1962, 30 Jan Arrived at La Spezia, Italy, for scrapping.
1962 June Demolition completed.

Liberté with her original funnels, as photographed in 1950 (*Roger Scozzafava*)

The domed funnel tops were added in 1954 and greatly increased the liner's mammoth appearance (*Roger Scozzafava*)

FLANDRE

Service Le Havre, Southampton (or Plymouth) to New York; winter cruising or Le Havre-West Indies service.
Particulars 20,477 tons gross; 600x80x26ft.
Builders Ateliers et Chantiers de France, Dunkirk, France, 1952.
Machinery Steam turbines geared to twin screw; service speed 22 knots.
Capacity 402 first class, 389 cabin class and 97 tourist class in 1952; 339 first class, 285 tourist class and 100 interchangeable after 1953.

1951, 31 Oct Launched.
1952, 23 July Maiden voyage from Le Havre to New York. Engine-room breakdown off New York; towed into port. Returned to builders for major overhaul.
1953, 17 Apr Commenced 'second' maiden voyage from Le Havre to New York.
1955 Apr Accommodation restyled as 232 first class and 511 tourist class.
1962 Oct Permanently assigned to Le Havre-West Indies service; repainted with a white hull.
1967 Summer crossings to Montreal for Expo 67.
1968 Feb Sold to Costa Line, Italian flag; renamed *Carla C*. Refitted for year-round cruise service: 19,975 tons gross; 754 one-class passengers.
1968 Dec Entered cruise service.
1969 Jan Began charter to Princess Cruises; Los Angeles-Mexico and Caribbean sailings.
1970 Returned to Costa for West Indies cruising from San Juan.
1974, 1 June Arrived at Amsterdam for conversion to motorliner.
1975 Jan Returned to service with new Stork-Werkspor diesels.

The smart-looking *Flandre* was enhanced further by a tapered funnel and electric cranes replacing conventional cargo gear (*F. R. Sherlock*)

As a cruiseship, *Carla C.* is painted in more tropical white (*Costa Line*)

FRANCE

Service Le Havre, Southampton, New York. Winter cruising.
Particulars 66,348 tons gross; 1,035x110x34ft.
Builders Chantiers de l'Atlantique, St Nazaire, France, 1961.
Machinery Steam turbines geared to quadruple screw; service speed 30 knots.
Capacity 501 first-class and 1,443 tourist-class passengers; 1,349 one-class during cruises.
Notes The longest liner ever built; last French Line transatlantic passenger ship.

1956, 26 July Ordered.
1957, 7 Oct Keel laid.
1960, 11 May Launched and named by Mme Charles de Gaulle.
1961 Nov Trial cruise from Le Havre.
1962, 3 Feb Left Le Havre on maiden voyage to New York.
1968, 9 Nov Completion of millionth sea mile; she had transported 412,097 passengers since 1962. Highly successful.
1969, 20 Nov First sailing to Bremerhaven; thereafter transatlantic crossings occasionally extended.
1972 Jan First world cruise.
1974 Sept Seized by union seamen and anchored in the Channel near Le Havre; surrendered to French Line officials on 9 October.
1974 Oct Withdrawn and laid-up near Le Havre.
1975 Sold to Saudi Arabian businessman Akram Ojjeh for $22 million. Proposed use as hotel-casino-centre of French culture failed to materialize. Ship remained idle at Le Havre.
1979 June Sold to Norwegian Caribbean Lines, Norwegian flag; renamed *Norway*. Sale price $18 million.
1979, 18 Aug Left Le Havre under tow for Bremerhaven, arriving there on 22 August.
1979 Aug Commenced major refit at Bremerhaven costing in excess of $40 million; restyled as year-round cruiseship. Only one engine room to be used, thereby conserving fuel: service speed of 16-18 knots, maximum speed of 25 knots.
1980, 24 Apr Transferred by Hapag-Lloyd Shipyard to Norwegian owners; completion of refit. Gross tonnage relisted as 69,500, thereby becoming world's largest passenger liner. Passenger capacity increased to 2,181, all one-class; crew reduced to 800.
1980, 29 Apr Commenced special maiden Atlantic cruise: Oslo-Southampton-New York-Miami; arrived at New York on 16 May.
1980, 1 June First weekly 7-day cruise: Miami-Bahamas Out Island-St Thomas-Miami. Year-round cruise service.
1980, 19 Aug Immobilized in the Caribbean during power failure. Returned to port and repaired.

The *France* as she first appeared in 1962 with her noteworthy smoke-deflecting winged funnels. She was the last major liner designed to spend most of the year in transatlantic service (*French Line*)

As modified, the *Norway* undergoing sea trials in the North Sea during April 1980 (*Norwegian Caribbean Lines*)

The combination passenger-cargo ship *Nova Scotia* (*Alex Duncan*)

After being sold to Dominion Far East Line she was renamed *Francis Drake* and repainted with a grey hull (*Dominion Far East Line*)

Furness-Warren Line

NOVA SCOTIA

Service Liverpool to St John's, NF, Halifax and Boston.
Particulars 7,438 tons gross; 440x61x25ft.
Builders Vickers-Armstrong Shipbuilders Limited, Newcastle, England, 1947.
Machinery Steam turbines geared to single screw; service speed 15 knots.
Capacity 62 first class and 92 tourist class.
Notes Ice-strengthened hull.

1947, 2 Sept Left Liverpool on maiden voyage to Canada and Boston.
1961 Reduced to a 12-passenger freighter.
1962 Sold to Dominion Far East Line, Bahamian flag. Renamed *Francis Drake*: 130 first-class passengers. Australia-Far East-Japan service.
1971, 16 Mar Arrived at Kaohsiung, Taiwan, for scrapping.

NEWFOUNDLAND

Service Liverpool to St John's, NF, Halifax and Boston.
Particulars 7,437 tons gross; 440x61x25ft.
Builders Vickers-Armstrong Shipbuilders Limited, Newcastle, England, 1948.
Machinery Steam turbines geared to single screw; service speed 15 knots.
Capacity 62 first class and 92 tourist class.
Notes Ice-strengthened hull.

1948, 14 Feb Left Liverpool on maiden voyage to Canada and Boston.
1961 Reduced to a 12-passenger freighter.
1962 Sold to Dominion Far East Line, Bahamian flag. Renamed *George Anson*: 130 first-class passengers. Australia-Far East-Japan service.
1971, 15 Feb Arrived at Kaohsiung, Taiwan, for scrapping.

Hanseatic anchored at Malta during a Mediterranean cruise (*Michael Cassar*)

German-Atlantic Line

HANSEATIC

Service Cuxhaven (Hamburg), Southampton, New York; winter cruising.
Particulars 25,338 tons gross; 629x82x26ft.
Builders Chantiers de l'Atlantique, St Nazaire, France, 1964.
Machinery Steam turbines geared to twin screw; service speed 20 knots.
Capacity 148 first class and 864 tourist class; 650 one-class for cruising.

1967 May Acquired from Zim Lines as *Shalom* (qv).
1967 Nov Formally transferred to German-Atlantic Line.
1967 Dec Maiden cruise as *Hanseatic*.
1967-9 Cuxhaven-Southampton-New York sailings and cruises.
1969-73 Cruising only.
1973 Aug Sold to Home Lines.
1973, 25 Sept Transferred at Genoa; renamed *Doric*, Panamanian flag. Refitted: 945 one-class cruise passengers.
1974 Jan Entered winter cruise service from Port Everglades to the Caribbean; summers between New York and Bermuda.
1981 Jan Sold to Royal Cruise Lines, Greek flag; for delivery in February 1982. To be refitted and renamed *Royal Odyssey*. Summer Scandinavian cruising, and Mediterranean and Caribbean sailings.

Hamburg arriving at Los Angeles following a Pacific cruise (*German-Atlantic Line*)

HAMBURG

Service Occasional 'positioning' voyages between Cuxhaven, Southampton and New York; mostly cruising.
Particulars 24,962 tons gross; 642x90ft.
Builders Deutsche Werft Shipyard, Hamburg, West Germany, 1969.
Machinery Steam turbines geared to twin screw; service speed 21 knots.
Capacity 600 one-class passengers; 790 at maximum.
Notes West Germany's first newly built post-war passenger liner.

1966, 1 Apr Ordered.
1968, 21 Feb Launched: intended for summer service Cuxhaven-Southampton-New York and off-season cruising. Near completion, operations revised to year-round cruising.
1969 Jan Delayed by turbine problems.
1969 Mar Delivered.
1969, 30 Mar Maiden cruise Cuxhaven-South America.
1969 June Maiden sailing to New York.
1972, 7 Feb Commenced cruise service from San Francisco and Los Angeles.
1973 Sept Renamed *Hanseatic* for further cruising.
1973 Dec Withdrawn from service; laid-up. Reportedly sold to Ryutsu Kaiun K.K., Japan, for £11 million. Sale collapsed. Then sold to Robin International, Liberia, as agents for Black Sea Steamship Company, Odessa; renamed *Maxim Gorky*, Soviet flag.
1974, 19 Feb Left Southampton under charter to United Artists Films as floating prop for film 'Juggernaut'; temporarily renamed *Britannic*.
1974-5 Cruising from New York.
1975 Nov Damaged by bomb explosion at San Juan.
1975 Dec Transferred to European cruising.

The former Australian coastal passenger ship *Canberra*, which spent six years on the North Atlantic for the Greek Line (*Alex Duncan*)

Greek Line _____

CANBERRA

Service Bremerhaven, Southampton, Cherbourg, Cobh, Montreal; laid-up during the winter season.
Particulars 7,707 tons gross; 426x57ft.
Builders Alexander Stephen & Sons Limited, Glasgow, Scotland, 1913.
Machinery Quadruple-expansion engines geared to twin screw; service speed 15 knots.
Capacity 64 first class and 646 tourist class.

1913 Completed as *Canberra* for Australian Steamships Proprietary Limited for the Queensland coastal trade.
1917-19 Used as a troopship.
1919-39 Australian service.
1939-45 Troopship.
1945 Laid-up.
1947 Reportedly sold to China; transferred at Singapore. Sale failed to materialize. Sold to Greek Line (Goulandris Group), Panamanian flag; retained original name. Mediterranean-Australia or Central America immigrant sailings.
1949 Refitted as an oil burner (formerly coal); entered Piraeus-Genoa-New York service.
1951 Commenced Bremerhaven-Southampton-Cherbourg-Cobh-Montreal sailings.
1954 Oct Final Greek Line sailing Quebec City-Bremerhaven.
1954 Dec Sold to Dominican Republican buyers; renamed *España*. Spain-West Indies immigrant service.
1959 Scrapped in the Dominican Republic.

Greek Line's *Columbia* had a career which spanned forty-six years (*Author's Collection*)

COLUMBIA

Service Mostly Bremerhaven, Southampton, Cherbourg, Cobh, Montreal; laid-up during the winter season.
Particulars 9,424 tons gross: 466x60ft.
Builders Harland & Wolff Limited, Belfast, Northern Ireland, 1913.
Machinery Combination triple-expansion engines and turbine geared to triple screw; service speed 15 knots.
Capacity 52 first class and 754 tourist class.

1913 Completed as *Katoomba* for McIlwraith & McEachern Proprietary Limited; Sydney-Fremantle service.
1915-18 Troopship.
1918-40 Australian service.
1940-6 Troopship.
1946 Oct Sold to Compania Maritima Del Este (Greek Line interests), Panamanian flag; sailed Sydney-Suez-Piraeus.
1946, 31 Dec Piraeus-Genoa-Oran-New York sailings.
1947-9 Chartered to French Line for Le Havre-West Indies service.
1949 Apr Refitted at Genoa: accommodation improved, renamed *Columbia*. Commenced Genoa-Australia sailings.
1950, 10 June Commenced Greek Line Atlantic sailings between Bremerhaven and Montreal.
1952, 31 Dec Damaged by fire at Bremerhaven.
1954 Transferred to Neptunia Shipping Company (Greek Line Interests), retaining Panamanian flag.
1957 Mostly Liverpool-Quebec City sailings.
1957, 18 July Fire at Quebec City.
1957 Aug Grazed by *Homeric* in fog.
1957 Dec Laid-up at Piraeus.
1959, 22 Aug Left Piraeus for Nagasaki, Japan, for scrapping.
1959, 29 Sept Arrived at Nagasaki.

After being purchased by Greek Line interests in 1948 *Neptunia*'s second funnel and mainmast were removed (*Greek Line*)

Neptunia, as painted with a white hull (*Alex Duncan*)

NEPTUNIA

Service Piraeus-Genoa-New York (1949-51); Bremerhaven-Southampton-Cherbourg-New York (1951-5); Bremerhaven-Southampton-Quebec City-Montreal (1955-7). Occasional winter cruising.
Particulars 10,519 tons gross; 523x59ft.
Builders Netherlands Shipbuilding Company, Amsterdam, Holland, 1920.
Machinery Triple-expansion engines geared to twin screw; service speed 15 knots.
Capacity 39 first class and 748 tourist class.

1919, 2 May Launched.
1920 July Completed as *Johan de Witt* for Nederland Line, Dutch flag. Amsterdam-East Indies service; 197 first class, 120 second class and 36 third class.
1930 Dec-1932 Nov Laid-up owing to the Depression.
1932 Nov Reactivated.
1933 Apr-Oct Major overhaul at Amsterdam; length increased from 499 to 523ft.
1940 Laid-up for safety in the Dutch East Indies. Later refitted as a troopship at Sydney; wartime management by British-flag Orient Line.
1945 Decommissioned; laid-up.
1948, 15 Dec Sold to Compania Maritima Del Este (Greek Line interests), Panamanian flag; renamed *Neptunia*. Major refit: second funnel removed as well as mainmast, accommodation revised to 39 first class and 748 tourist class.
1949 Piraeus-Genoa-New York sailings.
1951, 8 Apr Commenced New York-Cherbourg-Southampton-Bremerhaven service.
1954 Transferred to Neptunia Shipping Company (Greek Line interests), retaining Panamanian registry.
1955 Apr Commenced Bremerhaven-Southampton-Quebec City-Montreal sailings.
1957, 2 Nov Struck Daunts Rock, near Cobh; beached. Total loss.
1958, 2 Mar Towed to Rotterdam for scrapping.

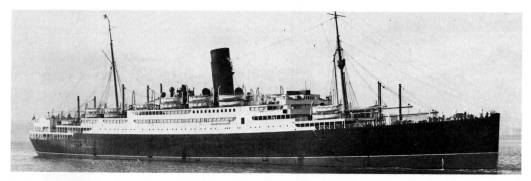

Anchor Line's *Tuscania* as photographed at Liverpool in the early 1930s (*David E. Pettit Collection*)

As *New York* she is shown departing from the port of the same name in 1955 (*Greek Line*)

NEA HELLAS/NEW YORK

Service 1947-54: Piraeus-Malta-Naples-Lisbon-Halifax-New York (Halifax and Malta omitted on eastbound sailings); 1955-9: New York-Boston (occasionally)-Cobh-Cherbourg-Southampton-Bremerhaven (westbound sailings included Halifax instead of Boston).
Particulars 16,991 tons gross; 578x70x29ft.
Builders Fairfield Shipbuilding & Engineering Company, Glasgow, Scotland, 1922.
Machinery Steam turbines geared to twin screw; service speed 16 knots.
Capacity 179 first class, 404 cabin class and 1,399 tourist class (1939-54); thereafter 70 first class and 1,300 tourist class.

1921, 4 Oct Launched as *Tuscania* for Anchor Line, British flag.
1922, 16 Sept Maiden voyage from Glasgow to New York; 240 first class, 377 second class and 1,818 third class.
1926-30 Chartered to Cunard Line for London-New York service.
1930 Oct-1931 Aug Laid-up owing to the Depression.
1931-9 Diverse operations: transatlantic crossings, cruises, Liverpool-Suez-Bombay service.
1939 Apr Sold to Greek Line; renamed *Nea Hellas*, Greek flag.
1939 May Commenced Piraeus-New York sailings; 179 first class, 404 cabin class and 1,399 tourist class.
1941-7 Trooping for the British Government.
1944, 12 Oct Aground at Glasgow.
1947 Refitted.
1947 Aug Resumed Piraeus-New York sailings.
1954-5 Major refit: renamed *New York*, accommodation restyled as 70 first class and 1,300 tourist class.
1955 Mar Commenced Bremerhaven-New York service.
1959 Oct Final Greek Line sailing Quebec City-Piraeus.
1959, 14 Nov Laid-up at Piraeus.
1961, 12 Oct Arrived at Onomichi, Japan, for scrapping.

Monarch of Bermuda with three funnels, as she was built in 1931 (*Roger Scozzafava*)

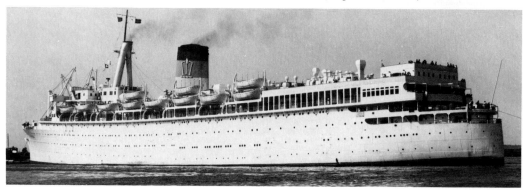

Vastly altered, the former *Monarch*, renamed *Arkadia*, with a new single funnel and smoke-dispensing dipod mast; note the long superstructure and the high stern-deck area (*F. R. Sherlock*)

ARKADIA

Service Bremerhaven-Amsterdam-London-Le Havre-Cobh-Quebec City-Montreal; occasional sailings to Boston. Cruising from Boston and from Southampton to the Canary Islands, Portugal and West Africa.
Particulars 20,259 tons gross; 590x84x26ft.
Builders Vickers-Armstrong Shipbuilders Limited, Newcastle, England, 1931.
Machinery Steam turbo-electric geared to quadruple screw; service speed 19 knots.
Capacity 150 first class and 1,150 tourist class; later changed to 50 first class and 1,337 tourist class.

1931, 17 Mar Launched as *Monarch of Bermuda* for Furness-Bermuda Line, British flag.
1931 Dec Commenced New York-Bermuda sailings; 22,434 tons gross, 830 passengers.
1939 Nov Became a troopship.
1947, 24 Mar Gutted by fire during post-war refit at Newcastle; hulk laid-up in the Firth of Forth. Later sold to the British Ministry of Transport and towed to Southampton. Completely rebuilt as the immigrant ship *New Australia*: one funnel, 20,256 tons gross, 1,600 one-class passengers.
1950 Aug Commenced Southampton-Sydney sailings, managed by Shaw Savill Line.
1958 Jan Sold to Greek Line. Major refit at Hamburg: tonnage revised to 20,259; accommodation restyled as 150 first class and 1,150 tourist class; lengthened from 579 to 590ft with new bow; renamed *Arkadia*, Greek flag. Entered Canadian service.
1959 Some cruising from New York to the Caribbean.
1961 Refitted at Hamburg: tonnage revised to 20,648; accommodation altered to 50 first class and 1,337 tourist class.
1966, 21 Nov Withdrawn; laid-up in the River Fal.
1966, 18 Dec Arrived at Valencia, Spain, for scrapping.

Originally designed as a freighter, *Skaubryn* was completed as an immigrant ship (*Michael Cassar*)

SKAUBRYN

Service Chartered to Greek Line for transatlantic sailings in 1957: Bremerhaven-Le Havre-Southampton-Quebec City service.
Particulars 9,786 tons gross; 458x57ft.
Builders Gotaverken Shipyard, Gothenburg, Sweden, 1951.
Machinery Diesels geared to twin screw; service speed 16.5 knots.
Capacity 1,205 one-class passengers.
Notes Former cargo ship.

1951 Mar Rebuilt as an immigrant ship by Howaldtswerke A/G, Kiel, West Germany; owned by I.M. Skaugen, Norwegian flag.
1951-7 Europe-Australia immigrant service.
1957, 18 June Commenced charter to Greek Line; Bremerhaven-Quebec City sailings.
1958, 31 Mar Caught fire in the Indian Ocean during Bremerhaven-Australia immigrant sailing; abandoned and then taken in tow.
1958, 6 Apr Sank while under tow.

Olympia was the first major liner to be built for Greek interests (*Roger Scozzalava*)

OLYMPIA

Service 1953-4: Bremerhaven-Channel ports-New York service. 1955-70: New York-occasionally Boston-Azores-Lisbon-Naples-Messina-Piraeus-occasionally Limassol and Haifa; westbound included Halifax instead of Boston. Mediterranean and Caribbean winter cruising.
Particulars 22,979 tons gross; 611x79x28ft.
Builders Alexander Stephen & Sons Limited, Glasgow, Scotland, 1953.
Machinery Steam turbines geared to twin screw; service speed 22 knots.
Capacity 138 first class and 1,169 tourist class.
Notes First major liner ever built for Greek owners.

1953, 16 Apr Launched as 'Number 636'. Intended name *Frederica*; dispute followed over Greek registry. Ship named *Olympia*, Liberian flag.
1953, 15 Oct Departed from Glasgow on maiden voyage to New York via Belfast, Liverpool, Southampton, Cherbourg, Cobh and Halifax.
1953, 14 Dec Ran aground at Southampton.
1954, 1 Mar Turbine trouble in the Caribbean during cruise.
1955 Mar Transferred to Piraeus-Mediterranean ports-New York service.
1961 June Turbine trouble off Halifax.
1961 Nov-Dec Major refit at Genoa.
1968, 27 Sept Transferred to Greek flag at New York.
1970 Major refit: 1,037 one-class passengers, cruising only.
1974, 24 Mar Laid-up at Perama, Greece; offered for sale.
1980 June Reported to have been sold to the Sheraton Hotel Corporation for use in 7-day Caribbean cruises from Miami as *Sheraton Caribbean*; scheme seems not to have materialized.

QUEEN ANNA MARIA

Service New York-occasionally Boston-Azores-Lisbon-Naples-Messina-Piraeus-occasionally Limassol and Haifa; westbound included Halifax instead of Boston. Mediterranean and Caribbean cruising.
Particulars 21,716 tons gross; 640x85x29ft.
Builders Fairfield Shipbuilding & Engineering Company, Glasgow, Scotland, 1956.
Machinery Steam turbines geared to twin screw; service speed 21 knots.
Capacity 109 first class and 1,145 tourist class; 900 one-class cruise passengers.

1956-64 Sailed as *Empress of Britain* for Canadian Pacific Steamships, British flag (qv).
1964 Feb Purchased from Canadian Pacific and registered by Transoceanic Navigation Company (Greek Line interests).
1964, 16 Nov Formal delivery; transferred to Greek Line, Greek flag.
1964-5 Refit at Genoa: passenger capacity increased from 1,054 to 1,254; tonnage revised from 25,516 to 21,716.
1965 Mar Renamed *Queen Anna Maria* by Her Majesty Queen Anne Marie of Greece.
1965, 24 Mar Left Piraeus on maiden voyage to New York.
1967, 19 Feb Grounded off Kingston, Jamaica, during cruise; refloated on 26 February.
1970 Cruising only.
1975, 11 Jan Left New York, thus ending Greek Line passenger service. Arrived at Piraeus on 22 January and laid-up.
1975 Dec Sold to Carnival Cruise Lines, Panamanian flag; renamed *Carnivale*.
1976 Feb First cruise from Miami to the Caribbean.

Queen Anna Maria arriving in New York on her maiden voyage in April 1965 (*Greek Line*)

As the Caribbean cruiseship *Carnivale*; notice the large outdoor deck areas (*Carnival Cruise Lines*)

Ascania at Southampton (*Michael Cassar*)

Grimaldi-Siosa Lines

ASCANIA

Service 1957-60 special transatlantic sailings from Southampton and Le Havre to New York or Quebec City.
Particulars 9,536 tons gross; 490x60x24ft.
Builders Ateliers et Chantiers de la Loire, St. Nazaire, France, 1926.
Machinery Steam turbines geared to twin screw; service speed 16 knots.
Capacity 87 first class and 1,160 tourist class.

1926 Completed as *Florida* for Transports Maritimes, French flag. France-Brazil-Uruguay-Argentina service.
1931, 1 Apr Badly damaged off Gibraltar in collision with aircraft carrier HMS *Glorious*; repaired.
1939 Commenced war service.
1942, 13 Nov Sunk by Nazi bombers at Bone, Algeria.
1944, May Refloated; towed to Toulon for refit. Second funnel removed.
1945 Returned to service.
1955 Sold to Grimaldi-Siosa Lines, Italian flag; renamed *Ascania*; refitted.
1955-6 Chartered to the French Government for trooping.
1957 May Began Le Havre-Southampton-Quebec City sailings.
1959 Further sailings to Quebec City.
1960 Plymouth-New York sailings.
1960-7 Southampton-Spain-West Indies service.
1967, 1 Oct Laid-up at La Spezia, Italy.
1968 Apr Scrapped.

Irpinia departing from New York during 1959 (*Grimaldi-Siosa Lines*)

IRPINIA

Service 1959-61: Genoa-Naples-Palermo-Gibraltar-Azores-Quebec City-Montreal service.
Particulars 12,279 tons gross; 537x67x23ft.
Builders Swan, Hunter & Wigham Richardson, Newcastle, England, 1929.
Machinery Steam turbines geared to twin screw; service speed 16 knots.
Capacity 187 first class and 1,034 tourist class.

1929, 11 June Launched as *Campana* for Transports Maritimes, French flag.
1929 Dec Completed for Marseilles-South America service.
1940 Laid-up at Buenos Aires for safety.
1943 July Seized by Argentine Government; renamed *Rio Jachal*.
1946 Returned to original owners; name reverted to *Campana*. Resumed South American sailings.
1955 June Sold to Grimaldi-Siosa Lines, Italian flag; renamed *Irpinia*. Major refit: lengthened from 527 to 537ft. with new bow; tonnage listed as 12,279; 187 first class and 1,034 tourist class. Entered Genoa-West Indies service.
1956 Oct Southampton-New York sailing.
1959 Apr Commenced Mediterranean-Canada sailings.
1962 Major refit at Trieste: new Fiat diesels fitted; two funnels replaced by one; 13,204 tons gross; accommodation restyled as 209 first class and 972 tourist class. Thereafter Southampton-West Indies service and cruising.
1970 Mar Cruising only.
1975 June Summer Scandinavian cruises from Tilbury
1976 Used as floating prop in film Voyage of the Damned .
1976 Thereafter cruises from Genoa.
1979 Reached fiftieth year.

Hamburg-Atlantic Line

HANSEATIC

Service Cuxhaven (Hamburg), Southampton, Cherbourg, New York. Winter cruising to the Caribbean from Port Everglades; also cruises from Cuxhaven.
Particulars 30,029 tons gross; 672x83x31ft.
Builders Fairfield Shipbuilding & Engineering Company, Glasgow, Scotland, 1930.
Machinery Steam turbines geared to twin screw; service speed 21 knots.
Capacity 85 first class and 1,167 tourist class.

1930-42 Sailed as *Empress of Japan*, Canadian Pacific Steamships, British flag.
1942-58 Sailed as *Empress of Scotland* (qv).
1958 Jan Acquired by Hamburg-Atlantic Line, West German flag, for £1 million; provisionally renamed *Scotland*, then formally as *Hanseatic*. Rebuilt at Howaldtswerke Shipyard, Hamburg, for £1.4 million. Three funnels replaced by two; accommodation increased from 708 to 1,252 passenger berths; new bow fitted, increasing length from 666 to 672ft; tonnage raised from 26,313 to 30,029.
1958 July Maiden voyage from Cuxhaven to New York.
1966, 7 Sept Seriously damaged by fire at New York's Pier 84; laid-up in Brooklyn shipyard. Towed to Hamburg for inspection, arriving 10 October. Beyond economic repair; sold to Eisen & Metall A/G, Hamburg, for scrap.

Hanseatic as rebuilt from the three-funnel *Empress of Scotland* (*Hamburg-Atlantic Line*)

Later in her career *Hanseatic*'s funnels were given stove pipes and dome grating (*F. R. Sherlock*)

Holland-America Line

VOLENDAM

Service 1947-51: 'austerity sailings' between Rotterdam and New York.
Particulars 15,434 tons gross; 579x67ft.
Builders Harland & Wolff Limited, Govan, Scotland, 1922.
Machinery Steam turbines geared to twin screw; service speed 15 knots.
Capacity Post-war: 1,693 one-class passengers.

1922, 6 July Launched.
1922, 4 Nov Maiden voyage from Rotterdam to New York via Boulogne and Plymouth; thereafter transatlantic service and cruising.
1940 Allied transport work.
1940 May Temporarily housed the exiled Dutch Government while at Falmouth.
1940, 30 Aug Torpedoed 300 miles off Ireland; taken in tow and beached. Eventually repaired at Birkenhead.
1941 July Returned to military work.
1945 July Returned to Rotterdam. Given partial refit, then chartered to the British Government for further trooping.
1946 Dutch trooping to Indonesia and immigrant sailings from Rotterdam to Australia.
1947 Further refit although never given complete restoration; passenger berths listed as 1,693 one-class. Commenced summer sailings between Rotterdam and New York.
1951 Nov Sold for scrap at Rotterdam.
1952 Feb Demolition began.

Veendam as she appeared in New York harbour in the early 1950s (*Roger Scozzalava*)

VEENDAM

Service Rotterdam, Le Havre, Southampton and New York; some cruising.
Particulars 15,652 tons gross; 579x67ft.
Builders Harland & Wolff Limited, Govan, Scotland, 1923.
Machinery Steam turbines geared to twin screw; service speed 15 knots.
Capacity 223 first class and 363 tourist class.

1922, 18 Nov Launched.
1923, 18 Apr Maiden voyage from Rotterdam to New York via Channel ports; thereafter Atlantic crossings and cruising; 262 first class, 436 second class and 1,200 third class.
1930 Chartered to Furness-Bermuda Line for New York-Bermuda sailings, then returned to Holland-America.
1940 May Caught at Rotterdam during the Nazi invasion. Later taken to Gdynia for use as a submarine tender and recreation ship for U-boat crews.
1945 Apr Found by the Allies at Hamburg.
1945 Oct Towed to Rotterdam; given major overhaul. Accommodation restyled as 223 first class and 363 tourist class.
1947 Jan First post-war sailing from Rotterdam to New York.
1953, 30 Oct Final sailing from Rotterdam to New York.
1953 Dec Sold to Bethlehem Steel Company for scrapping at Baltimore.

The very beautiful *Nieuw Amsterdam*, with her original black hull, arriving in New York in 1938 (*Roger Scozzafava*)

Repainted with a dove-grey hull, this aerial photograph shows the same ship on arrival in 1958 (*Holland-America Line*)

NIEUW AMSTERDAM

Service Rotterdam, Le Havre, Southampton to New York; winter cruising to the Caribbean.
Particulars 36,667 tons gross; 758x88x31ft.
Builders Rotterdam Drydock Company, Rotterdam, Holland, 1938.
Machinery Steam turbines geared to twin screw; service speed 21 knots.
Capacity 552 first class, 426 cabin class and 209 tourist class.
Notes Holland's flagship and largest liner 1938-59. One of the most popular and beloved of Atlantic liners.

1936 Jan Keel laid; to be named *Prinsendam*.
1937, 10 Apr Launched and named by Her Majesty Queen Wilhelmina as *Nieuw Amsterdam*.
1938, 16 May Maiden arrival at New York from Rotterdam.
1939 Sept Began cruising from New York to Bermuda and the Caribbean for safety.
1940 May Laid-up at Hoboken, New Jersey pier.
1940 Sept Acquired by British Ministry of Shipping for trooping; refitted at Halifax.
1946, 26 Apr Returned to Rotterdam and affectionately dubbed 'the Darling of the Dutch'; decommissioned from military duty with a war record of 378,361 passengers and 530,452 steaming miles.
1946-7 Major refit.
1947, 29 Oct Arrived in New York on first post-war voyage from Rotterdam.
1956-7 Major refit; repainted with dove-grey hull.
1961 Refit: accommodation restyled as 574 first class and 583 tourist class; tonnage revised to 36,982.
1965 Jan Rammed and sank a barge in New York Harbour.
1967 July Inspection revealed 'worn-out' boilers; rumoured that she would be scrapped.
1967 Sept Refitted instead with new boilers at the Wilton-Fijenoord Shipyard, Schiedam.
1971 Sept Terminated Holland-America's transatlantic service. Commenced two-month refit. Company restyled as Holland-America Cruises.
1971 Nov Based at Port Everglades, Florida, for year-round Caribbean cruises.
1972 Registered at Willemstad, Curaçao, instead of Rotterdam.
1973 Dec Final cruise.
1974, 2 Mar Arrived at Kaohsiung, Taiwan, for scrapping.

Noordam, outbound in New York's Hudson River (*Alex Duncan*)

NOORDAM

Service Rotterdam direct to New York.
Particulars 10,726 tons gross; 501x64x30ft.
Builders P. Smit Jr Shipbuilding, Rotterdam, Holland, 1938.
Machinery B&W-type diesels geared to twin screw; service speed 17 knots.
Capacity 148 first class.

1938, 9 Apr Launched.
1938, 28 Sept Maiden sailing from Rotterdam to New York.
1940 Mar Owing to war in Europe, ship transferred to New York-Dutch East Indies service.
1942 Apr Taken over by US War Shipping Board and used as a transport.
1946 July Resumed Rotterdam-New York sailings.
1963 May Withdrawn from Holland-America service.
1963 Sold to Cielomar S/A, Panamanian flag. Originally to have been renamed *Wallisien* but renamed *Oceanien* instead; chartered to Messageries Maritimes for their Marseilles-Panama-Sydney service.
1967 Sold to Brodospas.
1967, 14 Feb Arrived at Split, Yugoslavia, for scrapping.

The attractive-looking combination ship *Westerdam* as she appeared after 1946 (*Alex Duncan*)

WESTERDAM

Service Rotterdam direct to New York.
Particulars 12,149 tons gross; 518x66x31ft.
Builders Wilton-Fijenoord Shipyard, Schiedam, Holland, 1940-6.
Machinery MAN-type diesels geared to twin screw; service speed 16 knots.
Capacity 134 first class.

1940, 27 July Floated.
1940, 27 Aug Sunk in an Allied air raid; later refloated.
1944 Sept Deliberately sunk by the Dutch Underground to avoid use by the Nazi occupation forces. Refloated by the Nazis and then sunk again by the Underground.
1945, 13 Sept Refloated and refitted; completed.
1946 June Maiden voyage from Rotterdam to New York; first post-war Holland-America liner in service.
1964, 21 Nov Withdrawn from service.
1965 Jan Proposed that she should become a floating hostel for workers at the Royal Netherlands Blast Furnaces & Foundries plant, similar to *Arosa Sun* (qv).
1965 Feb Sold for scrap at Alicante, Spain.

Greatly altered by a new funnel device, *Ryndam* was renamed *Atlas* by the Greek-flag Epirotiki Lines in 1973 (*Michael D. J. Lennon*)

RYNDAM / WATERMAN

Service Rotterdam, Le Havre, Southampton to New York (until 1959) and to Montreal (from 1960); also cruising.
Particulars 15,015 tons gross; 503x69x28ft.
Builders Wilton-Fijenoord Shipyard, Schiedam, Holland, 1951.
Machinery Steam turbines geared to twin screw; service speed 16.5 knots.
Capacity 39 first and 836 tourist class.

1949, 17 Dec Laid down as the 60-passenger combination ship *Dinteldyk*; redesigned in early construction stages as a major passenger ship for transatlantic service.
1950, 19 Dec Launched as *Ryndam*.
1951, 16 July Maiden sailing from Rotterdam to New York.
1960 May Commenced new Rotterdam-Montreal service for Holland-America Line.
1964, 7 Nov Left Rotterdam on 'experimental trip' to Australia and New Zealand, then completely around the world.
1966, 14 Sept Transferred to Europe-Canada Line, West German flag. Atlantic student sailings and winter 'floating university' cruises.
1967 Oct Transferred to Transocean Steamship Company, Dutch flag.
1968, 24 May Renamed *Waterman* while docked at New York; student sailings.
1968, 9 Oct Returned to Holland-America; renamed *Ryndam*.
1971 Apr Reported sold to Sovereign Cruises, Greek flag; later cancelled. Laid-up at Rotterdam.
1972, 18 Aug Sold to Epirotiki Lines (Worldwide Cruises S/A), Greek flag, for $2.5 million; renamed *Atlas*. Thoroughly rebuilt for cruise service.
1973, 5 May Maiden voyage from Piraeus to the Aegean islands; 731 one-class passengers.
1980 Sept Reported sold to Viva Hotels, Mexican flag, for use as a Caribbean-South American cruiseship.

Maasdam departing from New York in 1963 (*Holland-America Line*)

MAASDAM

Service Rotterdam, Southampton, Le Havre to New York; later extended to include Bremerhaven, Cobh and (from 1966) to Quebec City and Montreal. Occasional cruising.
Particulars 15,024 tons gross; 503x69x28ft.
Builders Wilton-Fijenoord Shipyard, Schiedam, Holland, 1952.
Machinery Steam turbines geared to twin screw; service speed 16.5 knots.
Capacity 39 first class and 836 tourist class.
Notes She and sistership *Ryndam* were the first two-class liners with heavy tourist-class dominance.

1950, 19 Dec Keel laid; intended to be combination liner *Diemerdyk*.
1952, 5 Apr Launched.
1952, 11 Aug Special maiden voyage Rotterdam-Montreal-New York.
1963, 15 Feb Heavily damaged after striking two wrecks in Bremerhaven harbour.
1966 Assigned to Montreal service.
1968 Oct Sold to Polish Ocean Lines; refitted and renamed *Stefan Batory* (qv).

The handsome *Statendam* (*B. Reeves*)

STATENDAM

Service Rotterdam, Le Havre, Southampton, New York; off-season cruising.
Particulars 24,294 tons gross; 642x81x26ft.
Builders Wilton-Fijenoord Shipyard, Schiedam, Holland, 1957.
Machinery Steam turbines geared to twin screw; service speed 19 knots.
Capacity 84 first class and 868 tourist class.

1956, 12 June Floated in drydock; not launched. Named by Her Royal Highness Crown Princess Beatrix.
1957, 6 Feb Departed from Rotterdam on maiden voyage to New York.
1966 Cruising only, including sailings from San Francisco and Los Angeles.
1971 Sept-1972 Feb Given £2 million refit for cruising: 740 one-class passengers. Permanently assigned to New York cruise trade.
1973 Transferred registry from Rotterdam to Willemstad, Curaçao.
1974 Assigned to New York-Bermuda service and winter cruises from Port Everglades.
1981 May Commenced summer-season service from Vancouver to Alaska, 7-day cruises; continued winter sailings from Miami.

Rotterdam was the first Atlantic liner to dispense with the conventional funnel; exhausts were worked through the uptakes aft (*Holland-America Line*)

ROTTERDAM

Service Rotterdam, Le Havre, Southampton, New York; off-season cruising including annual voyage around the world.
Particulars 38,645 tons gross; 748x94x29ft.
Builders Rotterdam Drydock Company, Rotterdam, Holland, 1959.
Machinery Steam turbines geared to twin screw; service speed 20.5 knots.
Capacity Variable from 580 first class and 809 tourist class to 301 first and 1,055 tourist; 730 one-class during cruises.
Notes Holland's largest liner and flagship.

1956, 14 Dec Laid down.
1958, 13 Sept Launched and named by Her Majesty Queen Juliana; cost £13 million.
1959, 3 Sept Left Rotterdam on maiden voyage to New York.
1969 Cruising only.
1973 Transferred registry from Rotterdam to Curaçao.
1973, 28 Apr Commenced regular 7-day cruise service between New York, Bermuda and Nassau.
1973 Sept Repainted with dark-blue hull.
1981 Apr Commenced use of American West Coast as base of operations: summer sailings to Alaska; winter cruise around the world; occasional sailings from other ports.

The combination passenger-cargo ship *Prinses Margriet*, as painted in Holland-America colours (*Holland-America Line*)

PRINSES MARGRIET

Service Rotterdam direct to New York.
Particulars 9,336 tons gross; 456x61x28ft.
Builders De Merwede Shipyard, Hardinxveld, Holland, 1961.
Machinery MAN-type diesels geared to single screw; service speed 17 knots.
Capacity 111 first class.

1961-4 Sailed as *Prinses Margriet* for Oranje Line (qv).
1964 Dec Purchased by Holland-America; commenced Rotterdam-New York sailings.
1967, 15 Dec First sailing on charter to Royal Netherlands Steamship Company for 12-day cruises from New York to the Caribbean.
1970, 3 June Ended New York-Caribbean service.
1970 Sold to Nauru Local Government Council, flag of Nauru. Renamed *Enna G*; Pacific service.

The triple-screw passenger ship *Homeland*, which reached her fiftieth year in 1955 (*Roger Scozzafava*)

Home Lines

BRASIL / HOMELAND

Service Genoa-Naples-Palermo-Gibraltar-Halifax-New York or Hamburg-Southampton-Cherbourg-Halifax-New York.
Particulars 10,043 tons gross; 538x60ft.
Builders Alexander Stephen & Sons Limited, Glasgow, Scotland, 1905.
Machinery Steam turbines geared to triple screw; service speed 18 knots.
Capacity 96 first class and 846 tourist class.
Notes Reached fiftieth year.

1905-20 Sailed as *Virginian*, first for Allan Line, then Canadian Pacific Steamships, British flag.
1920-48 Sailed as *Drottningholm* for Swedish American Line, Swedish flag (qv).
1946 Mar Sold to Home Lines, Panamanian flag; delivery postponed until 1948.
1948 Transferred to Home Lines; renamed *Brasil*.
1948, 27 July Commenced Genoa-South America immigrant sailings.
1950 Apr Commenced Naples-Genoa-New York sailings.
1951 Major refit: renamed *Homeland*; tonnage revised from 10,249 to 10,043; accommodation restyled as 96 first class and 846 tourist class. Commenced Hamburg-New York sailings.
1952 Genoa-Naples-New York sailings.
1955 Mar Scrapped at Trieste.

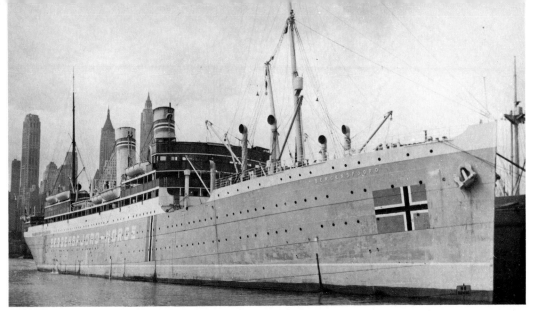

Norwegian America Line's *Bergensfjord* docked at Brooklyn, just opposite New York City, during 1940 (*Roger Scozzafava*)

Argentina was the first passenger ship in the very successful Home Lines fleet (*Home Lines*)

ARGENTINA

Service During 1952, Genoa-Naples-Palermo-Gibraltar-Halifax-New York.
Particulars 11,015 tons gross; 530x61ft.
Builders Cammell Laird & Company Limited, Birkenhead, England, 1913.
Machinery Steam turbines geared to twin screw; service speed 15 knots.
Capacity 32 first class, 969 tourist class.

1913, 8 Apr Launched.
1913 Sept Maiden voyage for Norwegian America Line, Norwegian flag, as *Bergensfjord*. Oslo-Bergen-New York service: 10,666 tons gross; 105 first class, 216 second class and 759 third class.
1920 Converted from coal to oil burner.
1931 Major refit at Bremen: new turbines fitted; passenger accommodation restyled as 367 cabin and 572 third class.
1938 Passenger accommodation again restyled as 90 cabin class, 155 tourist class, 500 third class.
1940, 15 Apr Arrived in New York; laid-up for safety.
1940 Nov Became Allied troopship: Norwegian crew, British management.
1946 Feb Returned to Norwegian America.
1946 Nov Sold to Home Lines, Panamanian flag; renamed *Argentina*. Refitted: tonnage relisted as 11,015; passenger accommodation revised to 32 first class, 969 tourist class.
1947, 13 Jan First sailing Genoa-South America.
1949 Sept Genoa-Central America service.
1952 Apr Genoa-Naples-New York service.
1953 Feb Sold to Zim Lines, Israeli flag; renamed *Jerusalem* (qv).

Matson Navigation's *Matsonia*, which worked the California-Hawaiian Islands trade (*Matson Navigation Company*)

The same ship painted in Home Lines colours as *Atlantic* (*Alex Duncan*)

ATLANTIC

Service 1949-51: Genoa-Naples-New York; 1952-4: Southampton-Le Havre-Quebec City. Winter cruising.
Particulars 20,553 tons gross; 582x83x29ft.
Builders William Cramp & Sons Ship and Engine Building Company, Philadelphia, Pennsylvania, 1927.
Machinery Steam turbines geared to twin screw; service speed 21 knots.
Capacity 349 first class, 203 cabin class and 626 tourist class.

1926, 26 June Launched as *Malolo*, Matson Navigation Company, American flag.
1927, 25 May During trials, collided with Norwegian freighter *Jakob Christensen* off Nantucket. Stayed afloat despite flooding with 7,000 tons of sea water; later repaired at Brooklyn.
1927 Nov Entered San Francisco-Honolulu service; 693 first-class passengers only.
1937 Major refit; renamed *Matsonia*.
1942 Feb Became United States Navy troopship.
1946 Apr Decommissioned and returned to San Francisco-Honolulu service.
1948 Sold to Home Lines, Panamanian flag. Refitted: passenger accommodation increased to 349 first class, 203 cabin class and 626 tourist class; renamed *Atlantic*.
1949, 14 May Maiden voyage for Home Lines on Genoa-Naples-New York service.
1952 Feb Commenced Southampton-Le Havre-Canada sailings.
1954 Dec Transferred to National Hellenic American Line, Greek flag; renamed *Queen Frederica* (qv).

Swedish-American's *Kungsholm*, photographed in 1940 with her neutrality markings (*Steamship Historical Society of America*)

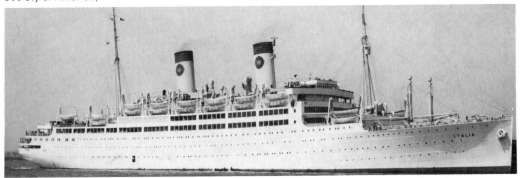

The same liner as Home Lines's *Italia* (*Alex Duncan*)

ITALIA

Service 1949-51: Genoa-Naples-New York; 1952-8: Cuxhaven (Hamburg)-Southampton-Le Havre-Halifax-New York; 1959-60: Cuxhaven (Hamburg)-Southampton-Le Havre-Quebec City-Montreal. Also cruising from New York to the Caribbean and Mediterranean.
Particulars 21,532 tons gross; 609x78x29ft.
Builders Blohm & Voss A/G, Hamburg, Germany, 1928.
Machinery B&W-type diesels geared to twin screw; service speed 17 knots.
Capacity 213 first class and 1,106 tourist class.

1928, 7 Mar Launched.
1928, 24 Nov Maiden crossing Gothenburg-New York as *Kungsholm* for Swedish American Line, Swedish flag; 20,223 tons gross; 115 first class, 490 second class and 970 third class.
1932-3 Refit; repainted with white hull. Gothenburg-New York service and cruising.
1942 Jan Became the American transport *John Ericsson*; sold to the War Shipping Administration, managed by United States Lines.
1947 Mar Damaged by fire at New York pier.
1947 July Resold to Swedish American Line.
1947 Dec Sold to Home Lines, Panamanian flag; renamed *Italia*. Refitted at Genoa.
1948, 27 July Left Genoa on maiden voyage for South America.
1949, 12 June Commenced Genoa-New York sailings.
1952 Mar Commenced Cuxhaven-Channel ports-New York service.
1954, 6 Oct Rammed and sank tug *Fairplay I* at Hamburg.
1959 Apr Commenced Cuxhaven-Channel ports-Canada service.
1960 Dec Refitted at Genoa: tonnage revised to 16,777; 680 first-class passengers only. Year-round New York-Nassau sailings.
1964 Apr Sold to Canaveral International Corporation, the Bahamas, for £446,000 for use as a floating hotel at Freeport, Grand Bahama Island. Renamed *Imperial Bahama Hotel*; given $1 million refit.
1965 Bankrupt; auctioned-off.
1965 July Sold to Spanish shipbreakers for £265,000.
1965, 8 Sept Arrived at Bilbao for scrapping.

HOMERIC

Service Cuxhaven (Hamburg)-Le Havre-Southampton-Quebec City-Montreal during April-November period; cruising from New York to the Caribbean during the remainder of the year.
Particulars 24,907 tons gross; 638x79ft.
Builders Bethlehem Steel Company, Quincy, Massachusetts, 1931.
Machinery Steam turbines geared to twin screw; service speed 20 knots.
Capacity 147 first class and 1,096 tourist class.

1931, 18 July Launched as *Mariposa*, Matson Navigation Company, American flag.
1932, 2 Feb Departed from San Francisco on maiden voyage to Honolulu, South Pacific ports and Australia; 734 passengers.
1941-6 United States Navy troopship.
1946-53 Laid-up at Alameda, California.
1953 Sold to Home Lines, Panamanian flag. Renamed *Homeric*; engines refitted.
1954 Sailed to Trieste. Major refit: passenger accommodation increased from 734 to 1,243 berths; tonnage listed as 18,563.
1955, 24 Jan Maiden voyage from Venice to New York; then Caribbean cruising.
1955, 3 May Maiden sailing Southampton-Canada.
1963 Oct Used for cruising only; 730 one-class passengers.
1964 New York-Nassau service.
1965 New York-Caribbean cruises.
1968 Sept-Oct Refitted at Genoa.
1973, 1 July Seriously damaged by galley and restaurant fire while outbound 90 miles off the New Jersey coast.
1973, 16 July Arrived at Genoa for inspection; beyond economic repair.
1974, 29 Jan Arrived at Kaohsiung, Taiwan, for scrapping.

Matson's *Mariposa* shown in the South Pacific in 1940 (*Matson Navigation Company*)

Home Lines's *Homeric* shown as a cruiseship (*F. R. Sherlock*)

Incres Line

EUROPA

Service 1950-1 Antwerp-Plymouth-New York.
Particulars 15,044 tons gross; 573x72x30ft.
Builders Sir W.G. Armstrong-Whitworth & Company Limited, Newcastle, England, 1923.
Machinery Steam turbines geared to twin screw; service speed 17 knots.
Capacity 500 one-class passengers.

1922, 14 Aug Launched as *Mongolia*, P&O Line, British flag.
1923, 11 May Departed from London on maiden voyage to Sydney: 230 first-class and 180 second-class passengers; 16,385 tons gross.
1931 Passenger accommodation restyled as 800 third class only; tonnage relisted as 16,956.
1938 Dec Commenced charter to New Zealand Shipping Company. Renamed *Rimutaka*; London-Panama Canal-Wellington service.
1940-9 Troopship.
1950 Feb Sold to Compania de Navigation Incres S/A, Panamanian flag. Renamed *Europa*; thoroughly rebuilt with 500 one-class passenger berths; tonnage relisted as 15,044.
1950, 5 July Commenced New York-Plymouth-Antwerp service.
1951 Oct Last sailing Antwerp-Plymouth-New York.
1952 Refitted as the cruiseship *Nassau*: 617 one-class passengers; tonnage 15,043. New York-Nassau year-round service; occasional transatlantic 'positioning' trips for overhaul and drydocking.
1954 Transferred to Liberian registry by Incres.
1961 Sold to Naviera Turistica Mexicana (Natumex Line), Mexican flag. Renamed *Acapulco*; first liner under Mexican flag. Refitted at Glasgow: lengthened to 575ft and tonnage relisted as 15,182.
1961 Dec Commenced cruising; Los Angeles-Mexico sailings.
1962 Used as a floating hotel at Seattle for World's Fair.
1963 May Laid-up at Manzanillo, Mexico, as uneconomic.
1964, 18 Oct Departed from Manzanillo in tow of the Japanese tug *Benten Maru* for Osaka.
1964, 15 Dec Arrived at Osaka for scrapping.

The former P&O liner *Mongolia* was renamed *Europa* for transatlantic service in 1950-1 (*Steamship Historical Society of America*)

The same ship as the cruiseship *Nassau*; notice the very extensive lido area with two outdoor swimming pools (*Incres Line*)

The British-flag *Dunnottar Castle* as built in 1936 (*Alex Duncan*)

Hardly recognizable, yet the same ship as the sleek *Victoria*. Note the mast attached to the funnel (*F. R. Sherlock*)

VICTORIA

Service Annual transatlantic 'positioning' New York-Genoa and New York-Southampton-Amsterdam. Year-round cruising to the Caribbean from New York.
Particulars 14,917 tons gross; 573x72x28ft.
Builders Harland & Wolff Limited, Belfast, Northern Ireland, 1936.
Machinery Fiat-type diesels geared to twin screw; service speed 18 knots.
Capacity 600 one-class passengers.

1936, 25 Jan Launched as *Dunnottar Castle*, Union Castle Line, British flag.
1936 July Maiden voyage Southampton-Capetown; then on London-around-Africa service. 15,007 tons gross; 258 first-class and 250 tourist-class passengers.
1939 Oct Became an armed merchant cruiser.
1942 Became a troopship.
1948 Decommissioned from war duties. Major refit: tonnage revised to 15,054; passenger accommodation restyled as 105 first class and 263 tourist class.
1949 Feb Returned to London-around-Africa service.
1958 Withdrawn and laid-up. Sold to Incres Steamship Company, Liberia; renamed *Victoria*. Towed to Schiedam, Holland, and totally rebuilt: given new Fiat diesels replacing original B&W diesels; accommodation rebuilt as 600 one-class.
1960 Jan Maiden voyage Le Havre-New York; then Caribbean cruising.
1964 Ownership transferred to Victoria Steamship Company, Liberian flag; continued under Incres operation.
1975 Aug Laid-up at New York following bankruptcy of Incres.
1975 Nov Sold to Chandris Group, Greek flag; retained name.
1976 June Began Mediterranean and Black Sea cruising.
1977 Transferred to ownership of Phaidon Navigation S/A (Chandris Group), Panamanian flag. Renamed *The Victoria*; Mediterranean and Caribbean cruising.
1980 July Refit with 46 cabins added.
1981 May Began summer cruises from Amsterdam to Scandinavia.

The wartime troopship *Hermitage*, formerly *Conte Biancamano*, resting in drydock at San Francisco in 1945 (*Frank O. Braynard Collection*)

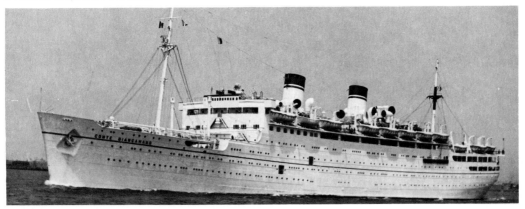

In peacetime Italian Line colours (*Roger Scozzafava*)

Italian Line

CONTE BIANCAMANO

Service Genoa-Cannes-Naples-Palermo-Gibraltar-Halifax (westbound only)-New York; stop at Boston (eastbound only). Winter service from Genoa to South America.
Particulars 23,842 tons gross; 665x76x26ft.
Builders William Beardmore & Company, Glasgow, Scotland, 1925.
Machinery Steam turbines geared to twin screw; service speed 18 knots.
Capacity 215 first class, 333 cabin class and 1,030 tourist class.

1925, 23 Apr Launched.
1925 Nov Completed for Lloyd Sabaudo, Italian flag; named *Conte Biancamano*. Genoa-New York service.
1932 Transferred to Italian Line; Genoa-South America service.
1937 Transferred to Lloyd Triestino; Genoa-Far East service.
1939 Transferred to Italian Line; Genoa-South America service.
1941 Dec Seized by the US Government at Cristobal; refitted as the troopship *Hermitage*.
1946 Aug Decommissioned.
1947 Aug Returned to Italy; renamed *Conte Biancamano*; major refit.
1949, 10 Nov Commenced Genoa-South America service. Ship owned by Società Maritima Nazionale and chartered to Italian Line.
1950-9 Summer-season service to New York.
1960 Apr Laid-up at Naples.
1960, 16 Aug Arrived at La Spezia for scrapping.

Conte Grande as she appeared during the 1930s (*Eric Johnson*)

Again the *Conte* but photographed in 1955 at Genoa (*F. R. Sherlock*)

CONTE GRANDE

Service Genoa-Cannes-Naples-Palermo-Gibraltar-Halifax (westbound only)-New York, summer only; otherwise Genoa-South America service.
Particulars 23,562 tons gross; 667x78x27ft.
Builders Stablimento Tecnico, Trieste, Italy, 1928.
Machinery Steam turbines geared to twin screw; service speed 18 knots.
Capacity 261 first class, 338 cabin class and 780 tourist class.

1927, 29 June Launched.
1928 Apr Completed for Lloyd Sabaudo, Italian flag, as *Conte Grande*; Genoa-New York service.
1932 Transferred to Italian Line.
1933 Transferred to Genoa-South America service.
1940 Laid-up at Santos.
1941, 22 Aug Seized by the US Government at Santos. Refitted as a troopship; renamed *Monticello*.
1946, 22 Mar Decommissioned from war duties.
1947, 23 July Returned to Italy; reverted to name *Conte Grande*. Major refit.
1949, 14 July Commenced Genoa-South America sailings; ship owned by Società Maritima Nazionale and chartered to Italian Line.
1956 Oct Final sailing to New York; thereafter South American sailings only.
1960 Dec One charter voyage to Australia for Lloyd Triestino.
1961, 7 Sept Arrived at La Spezia for scrapping.

Saturnia outbound from New York during the 1950s (*Steamship Historical Society of America*)

SATURNIA

Service 1947-55: Genoa-Naples-New York; 1955-65: Trieste-Venice-Patras-Messina or Palermo-Naples-Gibraltar-Halifax-New York; occasional calls at Boston, Lisbon, Barcelona and Dubrovnik.
Particulars 24,346 tons gross; 630x80x29ft.
Builders Cantieri Navale Triestino, Monfalcone, Italy, 1927.
Machinery Sulzer diesels geared to twin screw; service speed 19 knots.
Capacity 255 first class, 270 cabin class and 954 tourist class.

1925, 29 Dec Launched.
1927 Sept Completed as *Saturnia* for Cosulich Line, Italian flag. Trieste-South America service; 23,940 tons gross; 279 first class, 257 second class, 309 third class and 1,352 fourth class.
1928 Feb Transferred to Trieste-Venice-New York service.
1932 Transferred to Italian Line.
1935 Trooping to East Africa for the Italian Government.
1935-6 Original B&W diesels replaced by Sulzer diesels; service speed increased to 21 knots; tonnage relisted as 24,470.
1940 June Laid-up at Trieste.
1943 Sept Left Italy and taken over by the US Government for trooping.
1945 Jan-June Refitted as a hospital ship; renamed *Francis Y. Slanger*.
1945 Nov Decommissioned as hospital ship.
1946 Feb Returned to trooping.
1946, 1 Dec Returned to Italian Line; renamed *Saturnia*. Refitted.
1947, 29 Aug First post-war commercial sailing from Genoa to New York.
1955 Nov Transferred to Trieste-Venice-New York service.
1965, 11 Apr Laid-up at Trieste.
1965, 7 Oct Arrived at La Spezia in tow; sold to local scrap firm for £425,000.
1966 Apr Demolition commenced.

VULCANIA

Service 1947-55: Genoa-Naples-New York; 1955-65: Trieste-Venice-Patras-Messina or Palermo-Naples-Gibraltar-Halifax-New York; occasional calls at Boston, Lisbon, Barcelona and Dubrovnik.
Particulars 24,496 tons gross; 631x80x29ft.
Builders Cantieri Navale Triestino, Monfalcone, Italy, 1928.
Machinery Fiat-type diesels geared to twin screw; service speed 19 knots.
Capacity 232 first class, 262 cabin class, 958 tourist class.

1926 Laid-down, intended name *Urania*.
1926, 18 Dec Launched.
1928, 19 Dec Maiden voyage Trieste-New York for Cosulich Line, Italian flag, as *Vulcania*; 23,970 tons gross; 279 first class, 257 second class, 310 third class and 1,350 fourth class.
1932 Transferred to Italian Line.
1935 Trooping to East Africa for Italian Government.
1935 May-Dec Original B&W diesels replaced by Fiat diesels during major refit; tonnage increased to 24,469.
1941 Laid-up at Trieste.
1943 Sept Made a dash from Italy.
1943 Oct Became a US Army transport.
1946, 14 Dec Decommissioned by the US Government.
1947 Sept Resumed commercial sailings: Genoa-Naples-New York.
1955 Oct Commenced Trieste-Venice-New York service.
1965 May Laid-up at Trieste. Later sold to Grimaldi-Siosa Lines, Italian flag; renamed *Caribia*. Refitted: 337 first-class, 368 cabin-class and 732 tourist-class passengers.
1966, 12 Jan First sailing from Venice.
1966, 28 Feb Maiden sailing from Southampton to the West Indies.
1972, 29 Sept Laid-up at La Spezia.
1973 Jan Reportedly sold to Italian shipbreakers, then resold to Spanish shipbreakers.
1973, 18 Sept Arrived at Barcelona.
1974 Feb Resold to Taiwanese shipbreakers.
1974, 15 Mar Left Barcelona under tow for Kaohsiung.
1974 July Arrived at Kaohsiung.
1974, 20 July Sank in Kaohsiung harbour owing to leakages.

The low profile of the motorliner *Vulcania* is clearly evident in this photo (*Alex Duncan*)

During the early 1970s, as *Caribia*, the ship was cruising in the Mediterranean (*Michael Cassar*)

Giulio Cesare was the first major liner to be built in Italy after the War (*Alex Duncan*)

GIULIO CESARE

Service 1956-9: Naples-Genoa-Cannes-Gibraltar-New York; otherwise Genoa-South America service.
Particulars 27,078 tons gross; 681x87x28ft.
Builders Cantieri Riuniti dell'Adriatico, Monfalcone, Italy, 1951.
Machinery Fiat-type diesels geared to twin screw; service speed 21 knots.
Capacity 181 first class, 288 cabin class and 714 tourist class.

1950, 18 May Launched.
1951 Oct Maiden voyage Genoa-South America.
1956, 29 June First Genoa-Naples-New York sailing.
1960 Permanently on Genoa-South America service.
1964 Dec Became two-class ship: 181 first class and 1,000 tourist class.
1972 Dec Serious rudder trouble during Genoa-Buenos Aires sailing.
1973, 14 Jan Laid-up at Naples.
1973, 11 May Arrived in tow at La Spezia for scrapping.

Her sistership *Augustus* was equally as handsome (*Italian Line*)

AUGUSTUS

Service 1957-60: Naples-Genoa-Cannes-Gibraltar-New York service; otherwise Genoa-South America service.
Particulars 27,090 tons gross; 680x87x28ft.
Builders Cantieri Riuniti dell'Adriatico, Trieste, Italy, 1952.
Machinery Fiat-type diesels geared to twin screw; service speed 21 knots.
Capacity 180 first class, 280 cabin class and 714 tourist class.

1950, 19 Nov Launched.
1952 Feb Maiden voyage Genoa-South America.
1957, 7 Feb First Genoa-New York sailing.
1960 Permanently assigned to Genoa-South America service.
1964 Dec Became two-class ship: 180 first class and 1,000 tourist class.
1976, 16 Jan Laid-up at Naples.
1977 Sold to Great Shipping Investment Limited, Hong Kong; renamed *Great Sea*. Sailed to Hong Kong and laid-up; flag of the Seychelles. Offered for sale or charter.

The ill-fated *Andrea Doria* at anchor off Cannes (*Eric Johnson*)

ANDREA DORIA

Service Genoa-Cannes-Naples-Gibraltar-New York; some winter cruising from New York.
Particulars 29,083 tons gross; 700x90x30ft.
Builders Ansaldo Shipyard, Genoa, Italy, 1953.
Machinery Steam turbines geared to twin screw; service speed 23 knots.
Capacity 218 first class, 320 cabin class and 703 tourist class.

1951, 16 June Launched.
1953, 14 Jan Left Genoa on maiden voyage to New York.
1956, 26 July Sunk after collision with Swedish liner *Stockholm* off Nantucket; fifty-two casualties.

Cristoforo Colombo loading at Gibraltar (*Alex Duncan*)

CRISTOFORO COLOMBO

Service 1954-65: Genoa-Cannes-Naples-Gibraltar-New York; 1965-73: Trieste-Venice-Piraeus-Messina-Palermo-Naples-Halifax-New York-Boston-Mediterranean; occasionally included Lisbon and Barcelona.
Particulars 29,191 tons gross; 700x90x30ft.
Builders Ansaldo Shipyard, Genoa, Italy, 1954.
Machinery Steam turbines geared to twin screw; service speed 23 knots.
Capacity 301 first class, 242 cabin class and 703 tourist class.

1952, 19 Jan Laid down.
1953, 10 May Launched.
1954, 15 July Left Genoa on maiden voyage to New York.
1963 Jan Major refit: tonnage relisted as 29,429; accommodation restyled as 208 first class, 304 cabin class, 558 tourist class.
1965 June Transferred to Trieste-Venice-New York service.
1966 Aug Repainted with white hull.
1973 Feb Transferred to Genoa-South America service.
1977 Apr Sold to Venezuelan Government for £3.4 million for use as a floating hotel at Puerto Ordaz.
1977, 15 May Left Genoa for Mantanzas, Venezuela.
1978 Owners identified as CVG Siderogica Del Orinoco C/A, Venezuela.
1980 Feb Rumoured to be for sale.

Leonardo da Vinci was built as a replacement for the sunken *Andrea Doria* (*Michael D. J. Lennon*)

The same ship with a white hull after 1966 (*Alex Duncan*)

LEONARDO DA VINCI

Service Genoa-Cannes-Naples-Gibraltar-New York; after 1965, included other Mediterranean ports and occasional calls at Halifax (westbound) and Boston (eastbound); also cruising.
Particulars 33,340 tons gross; 761x92x30ft.
Builders Ansaldo Shipyard, Genoa, Italy, 1960.
Machinery Steam turbines geared to twin screw; service speed 23 knots.
Capacity 413 first class, 342 cabin class and 571 tourist class.
Notes Built so as to be converted to nuclear power.

1957, 23 June Laid down.
1958, 7 Dec Launched.
1960, 30 June Left Genoa on maiden voyage to New York.
1966 Feb Repainted with white hull.
1970, 27 Feb Left New York on a special 41-day cruise to Hawaiian Islands via Panama and the Caribbean.
1976 June Final Italian Line transatlantic sailing.
1977 July Transferred to Italian Line Cruises International. Miami-Nassau service: about 900 passengers one-class; operated by Costa Line.
1978, 23 Sept Laid-up at La Spezia; offered for sale.
1979, 4 June Suffered damage from burning freighter *Da Recco*, laid-up alongside.
1980 Jan Rumoured that she would be sold to the Trident Maritime Corporation, Panamanian flag, for Caribbean and South American cruises from New York and Port Everglades; plan never materialized.
1980, 3 July Swept by fire and burned for several days before being towed outside La Spezia and capsizing; total loss.

The latticed, winged funnels of *Michelangelo* became a standard recognition point for the ship (*Michael Cassar*)

MICHELANGELO

Service Naples-Genoa-Cannes-Gibraltar-New York; considerable cruising.
Particulars 45,911 tons gross; 902x102x34ft.
Builders Ansaldo Shipyard, Genoa, Italy, 1965.
Machinery Steam turbines geared to twin screw; service speed 26.5 knots.
Capacity 535 first class, 550 cabin class and 690 tourist class; 1,200 one-class for cruising.
Notes She and *Raffaello* were Italy's largest post-war liners.

1962, 16 Sept Launched.
1965, 12 May Left Genoa on maiden voyage to New York.
1965, 31 Dec First overhaul began: propellers changed; new trial speed of 31.59 knots.
1966, 12 Apr Struck by 50ft waves in North Atlantic storm; two killed, extensive damage.
1975 June Withdrawn and laid-up.
1975 Nov Reportedly sold to I.G. Tronado, Liechtenstein, for use as floating cancer-research centre; sale collapsed.
1977 Feb Sold to Iranian Navy.
1977, 8 July Departed from Genoa for Bandar Abbas, Iran, via Suez.
1977, 21 July Arrived at Bandar Abbas for use as an Iranian naval accommodation ship; 500 officers and 1,300 mariners.

Raffaello and her sister had considerable open-air spaces which included three swimming pools for adults and three for children (*Italian Line*)

RAFFAELLO

Service Naples-Genoa-Cannes-Gibraltar-New York; considerable cruising.
Particulars 45,933 tons gross; 902x102x34ft.
Builders Contieri Riuniti dell'Adriatico, Trieste, Italy, 1965.
Machinery Steam turbines geared to twin screw; service speed 26.5 knots.
Capacity 535 first class, 550 cabin class and 690 tourist class; 1,200 one-class for cruising.

1963, 24 Mar Launched.
1965, 25 July Left Genoa on maiden voyage to New York.
1965, 31 Oct Engine-room fire.
1970, 18 May Collision in Algeciras Bay with tanker *Cuyahoga*.
1971 Feb Rumoured to be transferred to Genoa-Buenos Aires service.
1975 May Withdrawn and laid-up.
1975 Nov Reportedly sold to I.G. Tronado, Liechtenstein, for use as a floating cancer-research centre; sale collapsed.
1977 Feb Sold to Iranian Navy.
1977 Aug Transferred to Bushire, Iran, for use as an accommodation ship for Iranian Navy; 500 officers and 1,300 mariners.

The former 'Victory' class freighter *Hrvatska* was converted to carry sixty one-class passengers in 1949 (*Michael Cassar*)

Jugolinija

HRVATSKA

Service New York (including stops at Baltimore and Philadelphia) to Casablanca, Naples, Trieste and Rijeka.
Particulars 7,904 tons gross; 455x62x28ft.
Builders Permanent Shipyard No 2, Richmond, California, 1945.
Machinery Steam turbines geared to single screw; service speed 17 knots.
Capacity 60 one-class passengers.
Notes Former freighter converted into a combination passenger-cargo ship.

1945 Mar Delivered as *St Lawrence Victory* to American War Shipping Administration.
1947, 25 Mar Struck a mine 8 miles off Dubrovnik; abandoned in sinking condition. Later towed by trawlers to Korcula and then to Split; claimed by Yugoslavian Government after being abandoned by American authorities. Renamed *Zagreb*; rebuilt with 60 passenger berths. Joined Jugolinija fleet.
1949, 20 Sept Left Rijeka on maiden voyage to New York as *Hrvatska*.
1967 Sold to Adab S/A of Geneva, flag of the African Kingdom of Burundi; later in same year sold to Compania Naviera Adriatica Limited, Costa Rican flag.
1968 Sold again to Société D'Avances Commerciales S/A, Somali Republic flag; renamed *Armelle*.
1972, 3 Sept Arrived at Bilbao, Spain, for scrapping.

The combination passenger-cargo ship *Srbija*, which was originally designed as a freighter for the German-flag Hansa Line (*Michael D. J. Lennon*)

SRBIJA

Service New York (including Baltimore and Philadelphia) to Casablanca, Naples, Trieste and Rijeka.
Particulars 6,634 tons gross; 475x60x25ft.
Builders A. Vuyk & Zonen, IJssel, Holland, 1949.
Machinery Sulzer diesels geared to single screw; service speed 15 knots.
Capacity 44 in first and tourist classes; later all one-class.

1944 Launched as *Crostafels* for German-flag Hansa Line.
1949 Completed as *Drvar*; shortly thereafter renamed *Srbija*.
1949, 17 Oct Maiden voyage Rijeka-New York.
1970 Reduced to a freighter; worldwide tramp service.
1980 Operating on Yugoslavia-Suez-Persian Gulf service.

VISEVICA

Service New York, Philadelphia, Newport News, Norfolk and/or Baltimore to Tangier, Casablanca, Valencia or Alicante, Genoa, Savona or Leghorn, Naples, Ancona or Sousse, Venice or Trieste, and Rijeka; ports determined by cargo requirements.
Particulars 6,750 tons gross; 492x65ft.
Builders 3 Maj Shipyard, Rijeka, Yugoslavia, 1964.
Machinery Sulzer diesels geared to single screw; service speed 18 knots.
Capacity 20 first class, 30 tourist class.

1966, 7 Feb Heavy damage during collision with United States Lines's freighter *Pioneer Myth* off the New Jersey coast; later repaired.

146

Jugolinija's combination-ship *Klek*. Accommodation is further aft than on most earlier passenger-cargo ships (*Michael Cassar*)

KLEK

Service USA-Mediterranean (same ports as for *Visevica*).
Particulars 6,750 tons gross; 492x65ft.
Builders 3 Maj Shipyard, Rijeka, Yugoslavia, 1965.
Machinery Sulzer diesels geared to single screw; service speed 18 knots.
Capacity 20 first class, 30 tourist class.

TUHOBIC

Service USA-Mediterranean (same ports as for *Visevica*).
Particulars 6,750 tons gross; 492x65ft.
Builders 3 Maj Shipyard, Rijeka, Yugoslavia, 1965.
Machinery Sulzer diesels geared to single screw; service speed 18 knots.
Capacity 20 first class, 30 tourist class.

1978 Assigned to freighter service Mediterranean-Venezuela-Central America-New Orleans.

ZVIR

Service USA-Mediterranean (same ports as for *Visevica*).
Particulars 6,750 tons gross; 492x65ft.
Builders 3 Maj Shipyard, Rijeka, Yugoslavia, 1965.
Machinery Sulzer diesels geared to single screw; service speed 18 knots.
Capacity 20 first class, 30 tourist class.

Khedivial Mail Line

KHEDIVE ISMAIL / CLEOPATRA

Service Alexandria to New York, Philadelphia and Baltimore via Beirut, Naples, Leghorn, Genoa and Marseilles; returning via Marseilles, Genoa, Naples and Beirut.
Particulars 8,193 tons gross; 455x62x28ft.
Builders Oregon Shipbuilding Corporation, Portland, Oregon, 1944.
Machinery Steam turbines geared to single screw; service speed 15 knots.
Capacity 100 first class.
Notes First 'Victory' ship built in America; former freighter converted to passenger-cargo liner.

1943, 13 Nov Keel laid.
1944, 12 Jan Launched as *United Victory* for War Shipping Administration.
1944, 28 Feb Completed; constructed in just over three months.
1946 Sold to Renfrew Navigation Company (Furness Withy & Company), British flag; commercial freighter service.
1947 Renamed *Khedive Ismail*.
1948 Transferred to Khedivial Mail Line, Egyptian flag; rebuilt with 100 passenger berths.
1948, 15 Mar Maiden sailing from Alexandria to New York.
1954 Began extended service that included India and Pakistan.
1956 Renamed *Cleopatra*.
1960 Transferred to United Arab Maritime Company, Egyptian flag. Route changed to Eastern Canada, Northern Europe etc, according to cargo requirements.
1975, 13 Nov Boiler explosion during a voyage from Hartlepool, England, to Alexandria; subsequently laid-up at Alexandria.

MOHAMMED ALI EL KEBIR

Service Alexandria to New York (same ports as for *Khedive Ismail*).
Particulars 8,199 tons gross; 455x62x28ft.
Builders California Shipbuilding Corporation, Los Angeles, California, 1944.
Machinery Steam turbines geared to single screw; service speed 15 knots.
Capacity 100 first class.
Notes Former freighter rebuilt as a passenger-cargo ship.

1944 June Completed as *Atchison Victory* for War Shipping Administration; 'Victory' class freighter.
1946 Sold to Renfrew Navigation Company (Furness Withy & Company), British flag.
1947 Renamed *Mohammed Ali El Kebir*.
1948 Transferred to Khedivial Mail Line, Egyptian flag; rebuilt with 100 passenger berths. Commenced Alexandria-New York sailings.
1954 Began extended service that included India and Pakistan.
1960 Sold to United Arab Maritime Company, Egyptian flag; renamed *Salah El Din*. Service according to cargo requirements.
1963, 4 Sept Swept by fire at Hamilton, Ontario.
1963, 22 Nov Towed to Quebec City.
1964 Sold to Salvador Investment Company Incorporated, Liberian flag. Renamed *Mercantile Victory*; repaired at Houston.
1964, 23 Apr Another fire; towed to Suez.
1964 Dec Towed to Marseilles; unrepaired.
1965 May Scrapped at Castellon, Spain.

Cleopatra and her sister were Egypt's only post-war Atlantic passenger ships; both were converted wartime
'Victory' ships (*J. K. Byass*)

A former aircraft carrier, *Sydney* was primarily an immigrant and low-fare tourist ship (*J. K. Byass*)

Lauro Line

SYDNEY

Service 1953: Liverpool-Quebec City sailings.
Particulars 14,708 tons gross; 492x69x27ft.
Builders Western Pipe & Steel Company, San Francisco, California, 1943.
Machinery Steam turbines geared to single screw; service speed 17 knots.
Capacity 94 first class and 708 tourist class.
Notes Auxiliary aircraft carrier converted into a passenger ship.

1941-2 Laid down as standard C-3 freighter. Redesigned as an auxiliary aircraft carrier; named *Croatan* by the US Navy.
1942, 9 Apr Launched. Transferred to the British Royal Navy: renamed HMS *Fencer*.
1943 Feb Entered service.
1943-6 War duties.
1946 Dec Returned to US Navy.
1946-50 Laid-up.
1950 Sold to Flotta Lauro (Lauro Line), Italian flag; renamed *Sydney*. Rebuilt at Genoa as an immigrant ship.
1951 Sept Entered Genoa-Australia service.
1953 Liverpool-Quebec City sailings.
1954-66 Genoa-Australia service.
1966 Genoa-West Indies service.
1967 Dec Renamed *Roma*; same owners; cruising only.
1969 Sold to Aretusa SpA, Italian flag, for cruising.
1970 Oct Laid-up at La Spezia.
1971 Jan Sold to Sovereign Cruises Limited, Cypriot flag, for $1 million; renamed *Galaxy Queen*. Refitted for Mediterranean cruise service: 900 one-class passengers.
1973 Sold to George Kotzovilis, Greek flag; renamed *Lady Dina*. Later resold to Marimina Shipping Company S/A, Italian flag; renamed *Caribia 2*.
1975 Feb Sold to Italian shipbreakers at La Spezia for 760 million lire.
1975, 1 Sept Demolition began.

The hull of *Roma* was that of a standard American C3-type freighter (*Roger Scozzafava*)

ROMA

Service 1953-6: Naples-Genoa-Barcelona-Gibraltar-Halifax-New York-Gibraltar-Genoa-Naples.
Particulars 14,687 tons gross; 492x69x27ft.
Builders Seattle-Tacoma Shipbuilding Corporation, Tacoma, Washington, 1943.
Machinery Steam turbines geared to single screw; service speed 17 knots.
Capacity 94 first class and 708 tourist class.
Notes Auxiliary aircraft carrier converted to passenger ship.

1941 Laid down as standard C 3 freighter.
1942, 7 Sept Launched as auxiliary aircraft carrier *Glacier*.
1943, 31 July Completed; handed over to the British Royal Navy; renamed HMS *Atheling*.
1946 Dec Returned to the US Government.
1947-50 Laid-up.
1950 Sold to Flotta Lauro (Lauro Line), Italian flag. Rebuilt at Genoa as a passenger ship; renamed *Roma*.
1951 Aug Maiden voyage Genoa-Australia via Suez with immigrants.
1953 May Commenced Mediterranean-New York sailings.
1956, 30 Nov Left New York on final transatlantic crossing.
1960 Major refit: passenger accommodation increased to 119 first class and 994 tourist class; tonnage listed as 14,976.
1966 Transferred to Genoa-West Indies service.
1967, 2 Nov Arrived at Vado, Italy, for scrapping.

Queen Frederica was christened as such in the presence of Her Majesty Queen Frederika of Greece (*Michael D. J. Lennon*)

National Hellenic American Line

QUEEN FREDERICA

Service Piraeus-Naples-Palermo-Gibraltar-Halifax-New York-Boston (occasionally)-Gibraltar-Naples-Palermo-Piraeus; winter cruising from New York to the Caribbean.
Particulars 20,553 tons gross; 582x83x29ft.
Builders William Cramp & Sons Ship and Engine Building Company, Philadelphia, Pennsylvania, 1927.
Machinery Steam turbines geared to twin screw; service speed 21 knots.
Capacity 132 first class, 116 cabin class and 931 tourist class.

1927-37 Sailed as *Malolo*, Matson Navigation Company, US flag.
1937-48 Sailed as *Matsonia*.
1948 Sold to Home Lines and renamed *Atlantic* (qv).
1954 Dec Transferred to National Hellenic American Line, Greek flag. Renamed *Queen Frederica*; refitted.
1955, 29 Jan Sailed from Piraeus to New York on maiden voyage; thence on 42-day Mediterranean cruise.
1960-1 Major refit at Genoa; tonnage relisted as 21,239; passenger accommodation restyled as 174 first class and 1,005 tourist class; 650 one-class for cruising.
1965 Nov Sold to Themistocles Navigation S/A (Chandris Group), Greek flag; retained same name (qv).

Zuiderkruis sailing from Capetown (*Alex Duncan*)

Netherlands Government

ZUIDERKRUIS

Service Summer-season sailings between Rotterdam and New York or Quebec City; occasionally via Le Havre and Southampton. At other times to Australia, South Africa and the Far East.
Particulars 9,178 tons gross; 455x62x28ft.
Builders Oregon Shipbuilding Corporation, Portland, Oregon, 1944.
Machinery Steam turbines geared to twin screw; service speed 16 knots.
Capacity 900 one-class passengers.
Notes Former freighter converted to passenger ship.

1944 May Delivered as *Cranston Victory* to War Shipping Administration, US flag; 'Victory' class freighter.
1947 Sold to Dutch Government for trooping service; renamed *Zuiderkruis*; managed by Royal Rotterdam Lloyd.
1951 Rebuilt as an immigrant ship at Netherlands Dock Company, Amsterdam: tonnage relisted as 9,178; managed by Nederland Line.
1951 July Maiden voyage Rotterdam-Quebec City; thereafter sailings to New York as well.
1960 Transferred to Trans-Ocean Steamship Company, Dutch flag. Refitted: tonnage relisted as 9,376; passenger accommodation restyled as 800 one-class.
1963 Jan Transferred to the Dutch Navy for use as an accommodation and stores ship at Den Helder; designated as A-853.
1969, 27 Nov Arrived at Bilbao, Spain, for scrapping.

The 'Victory' class transport *Costa Rica Victory* as built (*World Ship Society Photo Library*)

The same ship as the rebuilt passenger vessel *Groote Beer* (*Alex Duncan*)

GROOTE BEER

Service Summer-season sailings between Rotterdam and New York or Quebec City; occasionally via Le Havre and Southampton. At other times to Australia, South Africa and the Far East.
Particulars 9,190 tons gross; 455x62x28ft.
Builders Permanent Shipyard No 1, Richmond, California, 1944.
Machinery Steam turbines geared to single screw; service speed 16 knots.
Capacity 900 one-class passengers.
Notes Former freighter converted into a passenger ship.

1944 Aug Completed as *Costa Rica Victory* for War Shipping Administration, US flag; 'Victory' class freighter.
1947 Sold to the Dutch Government for troopship services; renamed *Groote Beer*; managed by Nederland Line.
1951-2 Converted to immigrant-tourist ship at Netherlands Dock Company, Amsterdam: tonnage listed as 9,190; 900 passenger berths installed; managed by Holland-America Line.
1952 July Maiden voyage Rotterdam-Quebec City-New York-Rotterdam.
1960 Transferred to Trans-Ocean Steamship Company, Dutch flag. Major refit; accommodation reduced to 800 one-class; tonnage revised to 9,384.
1963 Dec Sold to John S. Latsis Line, Greek flag. Renamed *Marianna IV* for local Mediterranean passenger service; tonnage listed as 9,892.
1965 June Chartered to Holland-America Line for summer student sailings to New York; renamed *Groote Beer*, Greek flag.
1966 Again chartered to Holland-America.
1966, 12 July Serious collision with sand dredger *Pen Avon* off the Needles Lighthouse, England.
1966 Sept Laid-up at Piraeus.
1967 Mar Laid-up in Eleusis Roads, Greece; name reverted to *Marianna IV*.
1970 June Scrapped at Eleusis.

Waterman at New York (*Roger Scozzafava*)

WATERMAN

Service Summer-season sailings between Rotterdam and New York or Quebec City; occasionally via Le Havre and Southampton. At other times to Australia, South Africa and the Far East.
Particulars 9,176 tons gross; 455x62x28ft.
Builders Oregon Shipbuilding Corporation, Portland, Oregon, 1945.
Machinery Steam turbines geared to twin screw; service speed 16 knots.
Capacity 900 one-class passengers.
Notes Former freighter converted to passenger ship.

1945 Feb Delivered as *La Grande Victory* to War Shipping Administration, US flag; 'Victory' class freighter.
1947 Sold to the Dutch Government for troopship service; renamed *Waterman*; managed by Royal Rotterdam Lloyd.
1951 Rebuilt as an immigrant ship: tonnage relisted as 9,176.
1952 Commenced Rotterdam-New York sailings.
1961 Transferred to Trans-Ocean Steamship Company, Dutch flag. Refitted at Flushing: tonnage relisted as 9,374; passenger accommodation restyled as 800 one-class.
1963 Dec Sold to John S. Latsis Line, Greek flag; renamed *Margarita*; local Mediterranean and pilgrim voyages.
1970 Mar Scrapped at Onomichi, Japan.

Remuera — the former Cunarder *Parthia* — as seen at London. Note the addition of a mainmast and one further lifeboat per side (*Author's Collection*)

New Zealand Shipping Company

REMUERA

Service 1963-4: eastbound sailings from Port Everglades to London via Bermuda as part of London-Panama-New Zealand-Tahiti-Panama-Florida-London sailings.
Particulars 13,619 tons gross; 531x70x30ft.
Builders Harland & Wolff Limited, Belfast, Northern Ireland, 1948.
Machinery Steam turbines geared to twin screw; service speed 18 knots.
Capacity 350 one-class passengers.

1948-61 Sailed as *Parthia* for Cunard Line (qv).
1961 Nov Sold to New Zealand Shipping Company; renamed *Remuera*. Major refit at Glasgow: tonnage altered from 13,362 to 13,619; passenger accommodation increased from 250 to 350 berths; mainmast added.
1962, 1 June Maiden voyage from London to Wellington via Panama.
1963 Commenced eastbound service from Port Everglades and Bermuda.
1964, 19 Nov Final New Zealand sailing. Sold to Eastern & Australian Steamship Company Limited; renamed *Aramac*; refitted at Hong Kong.
1965, 8 Feb Maiden voyage from Melbourne to Sydney, Manila, Hong Kong and Japanese ports.
1969, 22 Nov Arrived at Kaohsiung, Taiwan, for scrapping.
1970, 5 Mar Demolition commenced.
1970, 31 May Demolition completed.

Orient Overseas Line's *Oriental Carnaval* (ex-*Rangitoto*) laid-up at Hong Kong near the very end of her career. She and her onetime sister *Rangitane* ranked among the world's largest combination passenger-cargo ships (*Michael D. J. Lennon*)

RANGITOTO

Service 1963-9: eastbound sailings from Port Everglades to London via Bermuda as part of London-Panama-New Zealand-Tahiti-Panama-Florida-London sailings.
Particulars 21,809 tons gross; 609x78x32ft.
Builders Vickers-Armstrong Shipbuilders Limited, Newcastle, England, 1949.
Machinery Doxford-type diesels geared to twin screw; service speed 16.5 knots.
Capacity 436 one-class passengers.

1949, 12 Jan Launched.
1949, 25 Aug Maiden voyage London-Wellington via Panama.
1963 Commenced calls at Port Everglades and Bermuda.
1965 Mainmast removed.
1966 Adopted Federal Steamship Company colours.
1969 July Withdrawn and laid-up.
1969 Aug Sold to Oriental South America Lines (C. Y. Tung Group), Liberian flag; renamed *Oriental Carnaval*. Refitted: tonnage relisted as 19,567; 300 first-class passengers.
1970, 2 Dec Sailed from San Francisco on first around-the-world cruise.
1974, 9 May Terminated Orient Overseas Line's world-cruise service.
1975, 7 Mar Laid-up at Hong Kong.
1976 Feb Arrived at Kaohsiung, Taiwan, for scrapping.

The classic lines of *Rangitane* are apparent in this photograph taken just after her completion in 1950 (*New Zealand Shipping Company*)

RANGITANE

Service 1963-8: eastbound sailings from Port Everglades to London via Bermuda as part of London-Panama-New Zealand-Tahiti-Panama-Florida-Bermuda-London sailings.
Particulars 21,867 tons gross; 609x78x32ft.
Builders John Brown & Company Limited, Clydebank, Scotland, 1949.
Machinery Doxford-type diesels geared to twin screw; service speed 16.5 knots.
Capacity 436 one-class passengers.

1949, 30 June Launched.
1950, 27 Jan Commenced maiden voyage London-Wellington via Panama.
1963 Commenced eastbound calls at Port Everglades and Bermuda.
1965 Mainmast removed.
1966 Adopted Federal Steam Navigation Company colours.
1967 Transferred to Federal Steam Navigation Company.
1968, 6 May Withdrawn from service and laid-up; sold to Astroguarda Cia Nav, Greek flag. Renamed *Jan*; one outward voyage to Kaohsiung, Taiwan, presumably for scrapping.
1968, 11 Sept Arrived at Kaohsiung.
1969 Jan Sold to Oriental Latin America Lines (C. Y. Tung Group), Liberian flag; renamed *Oriental Esmeralda*. Refitted: tonnage relisted as 19,567; 300 first-class passengers.
1969, 4 June Left San Diego on maiden cruise around the world.
1976, 2 Apr Arrived at Kaohsiung, Taiwan, for scrapping.
1976, 21 June Demolition commenced.

Shown in San Francisco Bay, *Oriental Rio* (ex-*Ruahine*) was the largest passenger ship ever to fly the Taiwanese flag (*Orient Overseas Line*)

RUAHINE

Service 1963-8: eastbound sailings from Port Everglades to London via Bermuda as part of London-Panama-New Zealand-Tahiti-Panama-Florida-London sailings.
Particulars 17,851 tons gross; 584x75x29ft.
Builders John Brown & Company Limited, Clydebank, Scotland, 1951.
Machinery Doxford-type diesels geared to twin screw; service speed 16.5 knots.
Capacity 267 one-class passengers.

1950, 11 Dec Launched.
1951, 22 May Maiden voyage from London to Wellington via Panama.
1963 Commenced eastbound service from Port Everglades and Bermuda.
1965 Mainmast removed.
1966 Adopted Federal Steam Navigation Company colours.
1967 Transferred to Federal Steam Navigation Company.
1968 July Withdrawn and laid-up. Later sold to International Export Lines (C. Y. Tung Group), the Bahamas; renamed *Oriental Rio*. Later transferred to Chinese Maritime Trust (C. Y. Tung Group), Taiwanese flag; operated by Orient Overseas Line. Refitted: tonnage relisted as 17,730; accommodation restyled as 220 first class.
1969, 25 Feb Commenced first around-the-world cruise.
1973, 31 Dec Arrived at Kaohsiung, Taiwan, for scrapping

Berlin was West Germany's first passenger liner and in 1955 made the first German post-war commercial crossing (*North German Lloyd*)

North German Lloyd

BERLIN

Service Bremerhaven to New York; occasionally via Southampton and/or Halifax. In later years, annual sailing to Quebec City and Montreal; also cruising from New York and Bremerhaven.
Particulars 18,600 tons gross; 590x74x29ft.
Builders Sir W.G.Armstrong-Whitworth & Company, Newcastle, England, 1925.
Machinery B&W-type diesels geared to twin screw; service speed 16.5 knots.
Capacity 98 first class and 878 tourist class.
Notes The first German liner on the North Atlantic since 1939.

1925-54 Sailed as *Gripsholm* for Swedish American Line (qv).
1954, 1 Feb Began sailing for Bremen-America Line (a partnership firm of Swedish American and North German Lloyd); retained name. Bremerhaven-New York service.
1955, 8 Jan Maiden sailing as *Berlin* for North German Lloyd; Bremerhaven-New York service.
1966, 26 Nov Arrived at La Spezia, Italy, for scrapping; sold to the shipbreakers for £223,000.

The French troopship *Pasteur* with its giant funnel shown at New York in 1940 (*Steamship Historical Society of America*)

BREMEN

Service Bremerhaven-Southampton-Cherbourg-New York; winter cruising in the Caribbean from New York; also cruises from Bremerhaven.
Particulars 32,336 tons gross; 697x88x30ft.
Builders Chantiers de l'Atlantique, St Nazaire, France, 1939.
Machinery Steam turbines geared to quadruple screw; service speed 23 knots.
Capacity 216 first class and 906 tourist class.
Notes West Germany's largest post-war liner.

1938, 15 Feb Launched as *Pasteur* for Compagnie Sud-Atlantique, French flag; intended for the France-Brazil-Argentina service.
1939 Sept Maiden voyage from Bordeaux cancelled owing to threat of war.
1939 Sept-May Laid-up for safety.
1940-6 Troopship for the British Government; managed by Cunard-White Star.
1946-56 Peacetime trooping for the French Government, sailing mostly to Indo-China; capacity 4,000.
1957, 25 Jan Laid-up at Brest; offered for sale. Rumoured to be refitted for French Line transatlantic service.
1957 Sept Purchased by North German Lloyd. Renamed *Bremen*; sailed Brest-Bremerhaven for major rebuilding.
1957-9 Rebuilt at Bremerhaven: tonnage increased from 29,253 to 32,336.
1959, 9 July Departed from Bremerhaven on maiden voyage to New York.
1971 Dec Sold to Chandris Group, Greek flag, for $3 million; renamed *Regina Magna*; cruising only.
1972, 27 May Maiden Chandris cruise Amsterdam-Scandinavia.
1974, 17 Oct Laid-up at Perama, Greece.
1977 Sold to Philippine Singapore Ports Corporation, Philippine flag.
1977, 6 Oct Left Piraeus under tow for Jeddah for use as a floating hotel; renamed *Saudi Phil I*.
1977, 1 Nov Arrived at Jeddah.
1978 Mar Renamed *Filipinas Saudi I*; accommodation for 3,600 workers.
1980 April Sold for scrapping in Taiwan.
1980, 9 June Sank while being towed from Jeddah to Kaohsiung.

The modernized *Bremen* as seen in 1959 (*North German Lloyd*)

EUROPA

Service Bremerhaven-Southampton-Cherbourg-New York; considerable cruising from New York, Bremerhaven and Genoa.
Particulars 21,514 tons gross; 600x77x26ft.
Builders De Schelde Shipyard, Flushing, Holland, 1953.
Machinery B&W-type diesels geared to twin screw; service speed 19 knots.
Capacity 122 first class and 721 tourist class; later changed to 769 one-class.

1953-65 Sailed as *Kungsholm* for Swedish American Line (qv).
1965, 15 Oct Transferred at Gothenburg to North German Lloyd.
1965 Nov Renamed *Europa*; refit commenced.
1966, 9 Jan Maiden sailing from Bremerhaven to New York.
1970 North German Lloyd merged with Hamburg America Line to form Hapag-Lloyd; hull and funnels repainted.
1971 Transatlantic service discontinued; thereafter year-round cruising from Bremerhaven and Genoa.
1980 Oct Reported sold to Costa Line, Italian flag, with delivery in October 1981 for European and South American cruising.

Europa in the customary North German Lloyd colouring of black hull, white superstructure and mustard-colour funnels (*Michael Cassar*)

The same ship in cruising white with the new Hapag-Lloyd logo after 1971 (*Hapag-Lloyd*)

Norwegian America Line

STAVANGERFJORD

Service Oslo-Copenhagen-Kristiansand-Bergen-New York; occasionally included Halifax on westbound sailings.
Particulars 14,015 tons gross; 553x64x27ft.
Builders Cammell Laird & Company, Birkenhead, England, 1918.
Machinery Steam quadruple-expansion engines and turbines geared to twin screw; service speed 16.5 knots.
Capacity 122 first class, 222 cabin class and 335 tourist class; after 1956, revised to 90 first class, 172 cabin class and 413 tourist class.

1917, 21 May Launched.
1918 Apr Moved from the shipbuilder's yard to New York for safety.
1918 Sept Maiden voyage Oslo-Bergen-New York: 88 first-class, 318 second-class and 820 third-class passengers; 12,977 tons gross.
1924 Converted from coal to oil burning.
1931 Passenger accommodation restyled as 147 cabin class, 207 tourist class and 820 third class.
1938 Passenger accommodation modernized.
1939, 20 Dec Arrived at Oslo; laid-up.
1940-5 Used as Nazi troop depot ship; never sailed during the war.
1945 Aug First peacetime commercial Atlantic liner sailing: tonnage listed as 13,156; 122 first-class, 222 cabin-class and 335 tourist-class passengers. Oslo-Bergen-New York service.
1953 Dec Damaged and lost rudder in Atlantic gale.
1956 Nov-Dec Major refit: tonnage relisted as 14,015; passenger accommodation restyled as 90 first class, 172 cabin class and 413 tourist class.
1963, 14 Dec Final arrival at Oslo, having steamed 2,800,000 miles, made 770 Atlantic crossings, carried 500,000 passengers and reached 45 years of age. Sold to Hong Kong scrappers for $420,000.
1964, 2 Feb Arrived at Hong Kong for scrapping.

Stavangerfjord shown with her original thin funnels during the 1920s (*Mariners Museum*)

The same vessel as photographed in the late 1950s (*Norwegian America Line*)

The motorliner *Oslofjord* was for a time the largest passenger ship under the Norwegian flag (*Roger Scozzafava*)

OSLOFJORD

Service Oslo-Copenhagen-Kristiansand-Stavanger-Bergen-New York; considerable off-season cruising from New York.
Particulars 16,844 tons gross; 577x72x26ft.
Builders Netherlands Shipbuilding Company, Amsterdam, Holland, 1949.
Machinery Stork-type diesels geared to twin screw; service speed 20 knots.
Capacity 179 first class and 467 tourist class; 360 one-class for cruises.

1949, 2 Apr Launched by Her Royal Highness Crown Princess Martha of Norway.
1949, 26 Nov Left Oslo on maiden voyage to New York.
1957 Nov-Dec Refit: fitted with stabilizers.
1966 Jun Proposed sale to Finnlines; deal collapsed.
1966, 3 Nov Arrived at Amsterdam for three-month refit; made more suitable for cruising; tonnage relisted as 16,923.
1967, 22 Dec Began charter to Greek Line for cruises from Southampton.
1968 Sept Proposed charter to short-lived Ensco Shipping Company, British flag, for Liverpool-Montreal summer-season service during 1969; scheme abandoned.
1968 Oct Commenced three-year charter to Costa Line. Mediterranean cruises from Genoa during the summers and Caribbean cruises from San Juan during the winter season.
1969 Dec Renamed *Fulvia* by Costa.
1970, 20 July Sank off Tenerife after being abandoned following fire.

BERGENSFJORD

Service Oslo-Copenhagen-Kristiansand-Stavanger-Bergen-New York; considerable cruising during the off-season.
Particulars 18,739 tons gross; 578x72x27ft.
Builders Swan, Hunter and Wigham Richardson Limited, Wallsend-on-Tyne, England, 1956.
Machinery Stork-type diesels geared to twin screw; service speed 20 knots.
Capacity 126 first class and 752 tourist class; 420 one-class for cruising.

1954, 1 June Keel laid.
1955, 18 July Launched by Her Royal Highness Princess Astrid of Norway.
1956, 30 May Left Oslo on maiden voyage to New York.
1971 Apr Sold to French Line.
1971 Nov Delivered to French Line; renamed *De Grasse* (original intention was to rename her as *Louisianne*). Refitted. Le Havre-West Indies service and cruising; 580 one-class passengers.
1973 Sept Reportedly sold to Home Lines for $13.5 million; never materialized. Then reported as sold to Coral Riviera Limited of Tel Aviv for use as a floating hotel in Israel; again never materialized.
1973 Nov Sold to Thoresen & Company Limited, Singapore flag; renamed *Rasa Sayang*; refitted.
1974 Nov Commenced Singapore-Indonesia cruise service.
1977, 2 June Damaged by fire at sea and abandoned by passengers and crew.
1977, 4 June Towed to Singapore; repaired.
1978, 19 June Laid-up; offered for sale.
1978, 11 Dec Arrived at Piraeus after being sold to Sunlit Cruises Limited, Cypriot flag; renamed *Golden Moon*; laid-up at Perama.
1979 May Charter to Dutch travel firm for cruises from Rotterdam; intended to be renamed *Prins van Oranje*; never materialized.
1980 July Transferred to new Greek owners who planned to charter the ship to CTC Lines of London for winter cruises from Sydney to South Pacific ports; in preparation, renamed *Rasa Sayang*.
1980, 27 Aug Heavily damaged by engine-room fire while undergoing refit at Perama; towed to Kynosoura and sunk in shallow water.

The smart-looking *Bergensfjord* during a cruise in the late 1950s (*Norwegian America Line*)

As the Singapore-based cruiseship *Rasa Sayang* (*Michael D. J. Lennon*)

Sagafjord, which was originally intended to be named *Norway* (*Michael D. J. Lennon*).

SAGAFJORD

Service Some Oslo-Copenhagen-Bergen-New York sailings 1965-8; thereafter annual transatlantic 'positioning' voyages from New York and/or Port Everglades. All cruising.
Particulars 24,002 tons gross; 615x82x27ft.
Builders Société des Forges et Chantiers de la Méditerranée, Toulon, France, 1965.
Machinery Sulzer-type diesels geared to twin screw; service speed 20 knots.
Capacity 70 first class and 719 tourist class; mostly about 500 one-class for cruising.

1964, 13 June Launched; intended name was *Norway*.
1965, 2 Oct Began maiden voyage from Oslo to New York; ship owned 60% by Norwegian America and 40% by Leif Hoegh & Company.
1976 Nov-1977 Mar Temporarily laid-up.
1980 May Re-registered to Norwegian America Cruises.
1980 Sept-1981 Jan Major refit costing $12 million at Blohm & Voss Shipyards, Hamburg: addition of new top deck; change of engines and air-conditioning system; 15 cabins added.
1981 May Summer season 14-day cruises from San Francisco to Alaska and British Columbia.

Vistafjord docked at Oslo during her maiden voyage in May 1973 (*Michael D. J. Lennon*)

VISTAFJORD

Service Annual transatlantic 'positioning' voyages from Port Everglades and/or New York to Northern Europe or the Mediterranean.
Particulars 24,292 tons gross; 628x82x27ft.
Builders Swan Hunter Shipbuilders Limited, Newcastle, England, 1973.
Machinery Sulzer-type diesels geared to twin screw; service speed 20 knots.
Capacity 660 one-class passengers.

1971, 19 Apr Keel laid.
1972, 15 May Launched; cost £12.5 million.
1973, 22 May Left Oslo on maiden voyage to New York; thereafter all cruising.
1980 May Transferred to registry of Norwegian America Cruises; earlier plan to merge with Royal Viking Line had collapsed. Intention was to rename *Vistafjord* as *Royal Viking Vista* and *Sagafjord* as *Royal Viking Saga*.

Prins Willem van Oranje was the first ship in the Oranje Line fleet to carry more than twelve passengers (*Oranje Line*)

Oranje Line

PRINS WILLEM VAN ORANJE

Service Rotterdam-Southampton-Montreal-Chicago during the summer, ice-free months; to Halifax and Saint John, NB, during the winter.
Particulars 7,328 tons gross; 462x62x25ft.
Builders Boele's Shipbuilding & Engineering Company, Bolnes, Holland, 1953.
Machinery Werkspor-Lugt diesel geared to single screw; service speed 17 knots.
Capacity 60 one-class passengers.
Notes Ice-strengthened hull.

1953 Sept Maiden voyage Rotterdam-Montreal via Antwerp.
1959 June Began using the St Lawrence Seaway and sailing to Chicago and other Great Lakes ports.
1964 Reduced to 12 passengers.
1965 Feb Sold to V. E. B. Deutsche Seereederei, East German flag, for just under £500,000; terminated Oranje Line passenger service. Renamed *Ferdinand Freilgrath* for new owners.
1974 Renamed *Freijo* for unidentified new owners, then sold to Universal Shipping Corporation Incorporated, Panamanian flag; renamed *Universal Honolulu*. General tramp service.
1976 Renamed *August 8th*.
1977, 1 Oct Laid-up at Singapore.
1979, 20 Apr Arrived under tow at Kaohsiung, Taiwan, for scrapping.

Prinses Irene took part in the opening ceremonies of the St Lawrence Seaway in June 1959 (*Roger Scozzafava*)

PRINSES IRENE

Service Rotterdam-Southampton-Montreal-Chicago during the summer, ice-free months; Rotterdam-Southampton-Halifax-Saint John, NB, or to the Gulf of Mexico during the winter season
Particulars 8,526 tons gross; 456x61x28ft.
Builders De Merwede Shipbuilding Yard, Hardinxveld, Holland, 1959.
Machinery MAN-type diesel geared to single screw; service speed 17 knots.
Capacity 116 one-class passengers.
Notes Ice-strengthened hull.

1958, 12 July Launched by Her Royal Highness Princess Irene of Holland.
1959, 29 Apr Maiden voyage Rotterdam-Southampton-Montreal.
1959, 10 June Rotterdam-Southampton-Montreal-Chicago; took part in the official opening of the St Lawrence Seaway.
1964 Chartered to Cunard for cargo service to New York and other American East Coast ports.
1964 Dec Sold to Verolme Shipyards, Holland.
1965 Sold to Djakarta Lloyd, Indonesian flag; renamed *Tjut Njak Dhienn*. Refitted for the pilgrim trade: accommodation increased to 900 passenger berths.

Prinses Margriet was the third and last passenger ship to be built for the Oranje Line (*Oranje Line*)

PRINSES MARGRIET

Service Rotterdam-Southampton-Montreal-Chicago during the summer, ice-free months; Rotterdam-Southampton-Halifax-Saint John, NB, during the winter.
Particulars 9,336 tons gross; 456x61x28ft.
Builders De Merwede Shipbuilding Yard, Hardinxveld, Holland, 1961.
Machinery MAN-type diesel geared to single screw; service speed 17 knots.
Capacity 111 one-class passengers.
Notes Ice-strengthened hull.

1960, 10 Dec Launched by Her Royal Highness Princess Margriet of Holland.
1961 July Maiden voyage Rotterdam-Southampton-Montreal-Chicago.
1964 Dec Sold to Holland-America Line (qv).

Aboard *Orcades* the stovepipe atop the funnel with its black rim was known as the 'Welsh Hat'. She was the first P&O-Orient liner to be built after the war (*P&O-Orient Lines*)

P&O-Orient Lines

ORCADES

Service Periodically Southampton-Port Everglades via Bermuda and/or Nassau as part of worldwide passenger sailings; also cruising.
Particulars 28,396 tons gross; 709x90x30ft.
Builders Vickers-Armstrong Shipbuilders Limited, Barrow-in-Furness, England, 1948.
Machinery Steam turbines geared to twin screw; service speed 22 knots.
Capacity 631 first class and 734 tourist class.

1947, 14 Oct Launched; cost $9 million.
1948, 14 Dec Departed from Tilbury (London) on first voyage to Australia; cut passage time to Sydney from 36 to 26 days; 28,164 tons gross; 773 first-class and 772 tourist-class passengers.
1955 Aug Made first P&O-Orient liner voyage London-Australia via Panama Canal.
1959 Given complete air-conditioning during refit at Belfast; passenger accommodation restyled as 631 first class and 734 tourist class; tonnage relisted as 28,396.
1960 May Transferred from Orient Line to P&O-Orient Lines.
1964 May Converted to one-class ship: 1,635 passengers; tonnage relisted as 28,399.
1966 Oct Transferred from P&O-Orient Line to P&O Lines.
1970, 23 June Damaged off Fremantle during storm.
1972, 17 Apr Boiler-room fire at Hong Kong.
1972, 13 Oct Laid-up at Southampton.
1973, 6 Feb Arrived at Kaohsiung, Taiwan, for scrapping.

In the design of *Himalaya* the traditional mainmast was not used. Her funnel had a smoke-deflecting Thornycroft top (*P&O-Orient Lines*)

HIMALAYA

Service Periodically Southampton-Port Everglades via Bermuda and/or Nassau as part of worldwide passenger sailings; also cruising.
Particulars 27,955 tons gross; 709x91x31ft.
Builders Vickers-Armstrong Shipbuilders Limited, Barrow-in-Furness, England, 1949.
Machinery Steam turbines geared to twin screw; service speed 22 knots.
Capacity 758 first class and 401 tourist class.

1948, 5 Oct Launched.
1949, 6 Oct Maiden voyage from London to Sydney via the Suez Canal.
1958 Service extended to California and new around the world service for all P&O and Orient Line ships.
1959-60 Major refit in Holland.
1960 Transferred from P&O to P&O-Orient Lines.
1963 Dec Converted to one-class ship: accommodation restyled as 1,416 berths; tonnage relisted as 27,989.
1966 Transferred from P&O-Orient to P&O Lines.
1969 Remeasured at 28,047 tons gross.
1974, 28 Nov Arrived at Kaohsiung for scrapping.

Chusan was built specially for the England-Far East service rather than the Australian trade; at 24,000 tons she was the smallest liner in the P&O-Orient post-war rebuilding programme (*P&O-Orient Lines*)

CHUSAN

Service Periodically Southampton-Port Everglades via Bermuda and/or Nassau as part of worldwide passenger sailings; also cruising.
Particulars 24,215 tons gross; 672x85x29ft.
Builders Vickers-Armstrong Shipbuilders Limited, Barrow-in-Furness, England, 1950.
Machinery Steam turbines geared to twin screw; service speed 22 knots.
Capacity 475 first and 551 tourist class.

1949, 28 June Launched.
1950 July Maiden voyage; cruising from Southampton.
1950 Nov Commenced first London-Suez-Bombay-Yokohama sailing.
1959 Given major refit: accommodation restyled as 464 first class and 541 tourist class; tonnage relisted as 24,261.
1969 Cruising only; remeasured at 24,318.
1971 Oct Called at New York as part of a cruise from Capetown.
1973, 12 May Left Southampton for Taiwan.
1973, 30 June Arrived at Kaohsiung; later scrapped.

Oronsay pioneered the P&O-Orient passenger service to the North American West Coast in 1954 (*Alex Duncan*)

ORONSAY

Service Periodically Southampton-Port Everglades via Bermuda and/or Nassau as part of worldwide passenger sailings; also cruising.
Particulars 27,632 tons gross; 709x90x30ft.
Builders Vickers-Armstrong Shipbuilders Limited, Barrow-in-Furness, England. 1951.
Machinery Steam turbines geared to twin screw; service speed 22 knots.
Capacity 612 first class and 804 tourist class.

1950, 30 June Launched; cost $9.6 million.
1951 May Maiden voyage from Tilbury (London) to Australia.
1954 Jan Commenced P&O-Orient joint service across the Pacific to California and British Columbia.
1959 Given full air-conditioning during major refit.
1960 Transferred from Orient Line to P&O-Orient Lines.
1964 Repainted with white hull replacing original Orient Line biscuit colour.
1966 Transferred from P&O-Orient to P&O Lines.
1970, 14 Jan-4Feb Idle at Vancouver owing to outbreak of typhoid.
1975 Sept Withdrawn from service at Hong Kong.
1975, 7 Oct Arrived at Kaohsiung for scrapping.
1976, 10 Apr Demolition began.

In the late 1960s *Arcadia* did considerable cruising from California. She is shown in Glacier Bay, Alaska, during a summer voyage to the North (*P&O-Orient Lines*)

ARCADIA

Service Periodically Southampton-Port Everglades via Bermuda and/or Nassau as part of worldwide passenger sailings; also cruising.
Particulars 29,734 tons gross; 721x91x30ft.
Builders John Brown & Company Limited, Clydebank, Scotland, 1954.
Machinery Steam turbines geared to twin screw; service speed 22 knots.
Capacity 655 first class and 735 tourist class.

1953, 14 May Launched same day as Orient Line's *Orsova* (qv).
1954, 22 Feb Departed from Tilbury (London) on maiden voyage to Sydney.
1959 Major refit.
1959 Oct Entered trans-Pacific service to American West Coast.
1960 Transferred to P&O-Orient Lines from P&O Lines.
1966 Transferred to P&O Lines.
1970 Mainmast removed.
1975 Cruising from Sydney only.
1979, 29 Jan Departed from Sydney on final cruise.
1979, 28 Feb Arrived at Kaohsiung for scrapping.

Iberia was the final ship in the P&O-Orient rebuilding plan (*Schiffsfotos Hamburg*)

IBERIA

Service Periodically Southampton-Port Everglades via Bermuda and/or Nassau as part of worldwide passenger sailings; also cruising.
Particulars 29,614 tons gross; 719x91x30ft.
Builders Harland & Wolff Limited, Belfast, Northern Ireland, 1954.
Machinery Steam turbines geared to twin screw; service speed 22 knots.
Capacity 673 first class and 733 tourist class.

1954, 21 Jan Launched.
1954, 28 Sept Left London on maiden voyage to Sydney.
1956 Mar Collision off Ceylon with tanker *Stanvac Pretoria*.
1961 Major refit.
1969 Mainmast removed.
1969 Oct Difficult voyage: funnel caught fire at Pago Pago; electrical failure at Honolulu; engine difficulties at Acapulco, and fuel leak at Curaçao.
1971 Sept Refit.
1972, 19 Apr Laid-up at Southampton; sold to Mitsui & Company, Japan, for demolition in Taiwan.
1972, 16 June Sailed from Capetown for Kaohsiung.
1972, 5 Sept Arrived at Kaohsiung for scrapping.

Orsova was the first major liner to dispense completely with the ordinary mast (*Alex Duncan*)

ORSOVA

Service Periodically Southampton-Port Everglades via Bermuda and/or Nassau as part of worldwide passenger sailings; also cruising.
Particulars 28,790 tons gross; 723x90x30ft.
Builders Vickers-Armstrong Shipbuilders Limited, Barrow-in-Furness, England, 1954.
Machinery Steam turbines geared to twin screw; service speed 22 knots.
Capacity 694 first class and 809 tourist class.
Notes First major liner to dispense with the conventional mast.

1953, 14 May Launched.
1954 May Maiden voyage London-Sydney.
1955 July Completed first P&O-Orient around-the-world sailing, covering 46,000 miles.
1960 Refitted: given full air-conditioning. Transferred to P&O-Orient Lines from Orient Line.
1964 Repainted, with white hull replacing original Orient Lines biscuit colour.
1966 Transferred to P&O Lines.
1972, 25 Nov Began £225,000 refit at Southampton.
1973, 25 Nov Completed final P&O sailing; laid-up at Southampton.
1974, 14 Feb Arrived at Kaohsiung, Taiwan, for scrapping.
1974, 17 Dec Demolition began.

Oriana's maiden arrival at New York as part of a transatlantic cruise in August 1979 (*Moran Towing Company*)

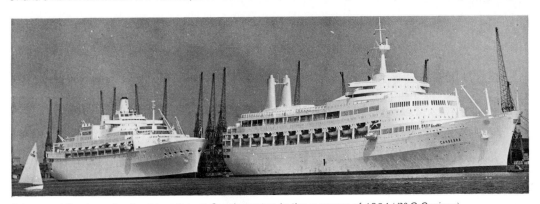

Oriana and *Canberra* berthed together at Southampton in the summer of 1964 (*P&O Cruises*)

ORIANA

Service Periodically Southampton-Port Everglades via Bermuda and/or Nassau as part of worldwide passenger sailings; also cruising.
Particulars 41,923 tons gross; 804x97x31ft.
Builders Vickers-Armstrong Shipbuilders Limited, Barrow-in-Furness, England, 1960.
Machinery Steam turbines geared to twin screw; service speed 27.5 knots.
Capacity 638 first class and 1,496 tourist class.
Notes The largest liner ever built in England.

1959, 3 Nov Launched by Her Royal Highness Princess Alexandra of Kent; ordered by Orient Line but completed for P&O-Orient Lines.
1960, 3 Dec Departed from Southampton on maiden voyage to Sydney; cut Southampton-Sydney passage time from 4 to 3 weeks. Fastest liner ever on the Australian run.
1966 Transferred to P&O Lines from P&O-Orient Lines.
1970, 17 June Boiler fire.
1970, 11 Aug Engine-room fire in Southampton Water off Fawley.
1973 Cruising only; transferred to P&O Cruises Limited; 1,700 one-class passengers; tonnage relisted as 41,915.
1979, 10 Aug Maiden North Atlantic cruise: Southampton-Reykjavik-Cornerbrook-Halifax-Boston-New York-Southampton.

CANBERRA

Service Periodically Southampton-Port Everglades via Bermuda and/or Nassau as part of worldwide passenger sailings; also cruising.
Particulars 45,733 tons gross; 818x102x32ft.
Builders Harland & Wolff Limited, Belfast, Northern Ireland, 1961.
Machinery Steam turbo-electric geared to twin screw; service speed 27.5 knots.
Capacity 556 first class and 1,716 tourist class or adjustable to 596 first class and 1,616 tourist class.
Notes The largest liner ever built for a service other than the North Atlantic.

1960, 16 Mar Launched; ordered for P&O Lines but completed for P&O-Orient Lines. Cost in excess of £15 million.
1961, 2 June Left Southampton on maiden voyage around the world.
1962-3 Some voyages to New York.
1963, 5 Jan Disabled by major engine problems off Malta; forced to return to Southampton and then to Belfast.
1966 Transferred to P&O Lines.
1973 Feb-Sept Based at New York for a series of 17 cruises; unsuccessful. Transferred to P&O Cruises Limited; 1,737 one-class passengers.
1973 Feb-Mar Temporary 'lay-up' at Wilmington, North Carolina.
1973, 12-15 July Aground off Grenada; refloated.
1973, 14 Aug Aground at the entrance to St Thomas harbour; refloated.
1973 Oct Cruising from Southampton only.

Canberra anchored at Valletta, Malta, during a Mediterranean cruise (*P&O Cruises*)

Polish Ocean Lines

BATORY

Service Gdynia-Copenhagen-Southampton (or London)-Quebec City-Montreal, from April to December; winter cruising from London to the Canary Islands, West Africa, Mediterranean and Caribbean.
Particulars 14,287 tons gross; 526x71x24ft.
Builders Cantieri Riuniti dell'Adriatico, Trieste, Italy, 1936.
Machinery Sulzer-type diesels geared to twin screw; service speed 18 knots.
Capacity 76 first class and 740 tourist class.

1935, 3 July Launched.
1936 May Maiden voyage Gdynia-New York: 370 tourist-class and 400 third-class passengers; also cruising.
1939 Sept Laid-up at Yonkers, New York, for safety. Later transferred to British Ministry of Transport; refitted at Glasgow for trooping.
1940-6 Trooping.
1946 Apr Commenced major refit at Antwerp.
1946 July Damaged by fire at Antwerp shipyard.
1947 Apr Returned to Gdynia-New York service.
1951 Jan Withdrawn from American service as a result of a series of political and labour problems, the most serious being the accusation that a spy escaped aboard the ship. Ship sent to Hebburn-on-Tyne, England, for a major refit; repainted with a grey hull.
1951 Aug Commenced new service Gdynia-Southampton-Gibraltar-Malta-Suez-Aden-Karachi-Bombay; also cruising.
1957 Jan-Aug Refit at Bremerhaven: accommodation restyled as 76 first class and 740 tourist class; repainted with black hull.
1957, 26 Aug Commenced Gdynia-Copenhagen-Southampton-Montreal service; occasional calls at London, Le Havre, Bremerhaven, Helsinki, Quebec City and Boston.
1965, 28 Dec Called at Boston, commencing occasional winter calls there.
1968 Dec Withdrawn from transatlantic service.
1969 Apr Withdrawn; sold to the Municipality of Gdynia for use as a floating hotel.
1971 Sold to Hong Kong shipbreakers.
1971, 11 May Arrived at Hong Kong for scrapping.

Batory in her original form during the 1950s with grey hull and the boats in Quadrant davits (*Alex Duncan*)

Following her 1957 refit the same ship was repainted with a black hull and all boats raised in Gravity davits (*F. R. Sherlock*)

Sobieski shown as the Soviet *Gruzia* (*Alex Duncan*)

SOBIESKI

Service Post-war 'austerity service' between Genoa and New York, 1946-50.
Particulars 11,030 tons gross; 511x67x26ft.
Builders Swan, Hunter and Wigham Richardson Limited, Newcastle, England, 1939.
Machinery B&W-type diesels geared to twin screw; service speed 16 knots.
Capacity 70 first class, 270 cabin class and 600 tourist class.

1938, 25 Aug Launched.
1939 May Maiden voyage Gdynia-Rio de Janeiro-Buenos Aires: 44 first class, 250 third class and 860 steerage class.
1940-5 Allied troopship.
1946-50 Genoa-New York service.
1950 Transferred to Sovtorgflot, USSR flag; renamed *Gruzia*. Used in Black Sea local service from Odessa; later, occasional voyages Odessa-Havana.
1975, 14 Apr Arrived at La Spezia in tow from Odessa for scrapping.

Stefan Batory at the time of her maiden voyage in April 1969 (*Polish Ocean Lines*)

STEFAN BATORY

Service Gdynia-Copenhagen-London or Southampton-Montreal; occasional calls at Rotterdam, Cuxhaven (Hamburg) and Quebec City; winter cruising from London to the Mediterranean, West Africa and the Caribbean.
Particulars 15,043 tons gross; 503x69x28ft.
Builders Wilton-Fijenoord Shipyard, Schiedam, Holland, 1952.
Machinery Steam turbines geared to single screw; service speed 16.5 knots.
Capacity 39 first class and 734 tourist class.

1968 Oct Purchased from Holland-America Line, formerly *Maasdam* (qv); thoroughly rebuilt at Gdynia.
1969, 11 Apr Left Gdynia on maiden voyage to Montreal; subsequently converted to 773 one-class passengers.
1981 Many transatlantic sailings terminating at Rotterdam rather than Gdynia.

Royal Viking Star was the first of the trio of cruiseships built for Norwegian owners for worldwide service (*Michael D. J. Lennon*)

Royal Viking Line

ROYAL VIKING STAR

Service Worldwide cruising; periodic 'positioning' voyages from New York and/or Port Everglades to Southampton, Copenhagen or to the Mediterranean.
Particulars 21,847 tons gross; 581x83x22ft.
Builders Wartsila Shipyards, Helsinki, Finland, 1972.
Machinery Wartsila-Sulzer diesels geared to twin screw; service speed 21 knots.
Capacity 539 first-class passengers.

1971, 12 May Launched.
1972 June Completed; commenced cruising. Owned by Bergen Line D/S, Norwegian flag, and operated by Royal Viking Line.
1979 Dec Plan to merge with Norwegian America Line collapsed.
1981, 28 Aug-Dec $25 million refit and lengthening at A.G.Weser Shipyard at Bremerhaven; to be increased to 29,000 tons and 700 passenger berths; length to increase to 674ft.

Royal Viking Sky's homeport is Trondheim, Norway (*Michael D. J. Lennon*)

ROYAL VIKING SKY

Service Worldwide cruising (same as for *Royal Viking Star*).
Particulars 21,891 tons gross; 581x83x22ft.
Builders Wartsila Shipyards, Helsinki, Finland, 1973.
Machinery Wartsila-Sulzer type diesels geared to twin screw; service speed 21 knots.
Capacity 536 first-class passengers.

1972, 25 May Launched.
1973 June Completed; began worldwide cruises. Owned by Nordenfjeldske D/S, Norwegian flag, and operated by Royal Viking line.
1982 To be lengthened with increased capacity, similar to *Royal Viking Star* (qv).

ROYAL VIKING SEA

Service Worldwide cruising (same as for *Royal Viking Star*).
Particulars 21,897 tons gross; 581x83x22ft.
Builders Wartsila Shipyards, Helsinki, Finland, 1973.
Machinery Wartsila-Sulzer type diesels geared to twin screw; service speed 21 knots.
Capacity 536 first-class passengers.

1973, 19 Jan Launched.
1973 Nov Completed for worldwide cruising; owned by A. F. Klaveness & Company A/S, Norwegian flag. Since sold and is now owned jointly by Bergen Line and Nordenfjeldske. Initially made five North Sea crossings between Bergen and Newcastle for Bergen Line.
1983 To be lengthened with increased capacity, similar to *Royal Viking Star* (qv).

Southern Cross was the first major liner to have her engines so far aft (*Shaw Savill Line*)

As *Calypso*, she was repainted with a white hull and given a rather distinctive funnel colouring (*Michael D. J. Lennon*)

Shaw Savill Line

SOUTHERN CROSS

Service Occasional Southampton-Port Everglades sailings via Bermuda as part of full around-the-world service; Southampton-Bermuda-Port Everglades-Trinidad-Curaçao-Panama Canal-Tahiti-Fiji-Wellington-Auckland-Sydney-Melbourne-Fremantle-Durban-Capetown-Las Palmas-Southampton.
Particulars 20,204 tons gross; 604x78x25ft.
Builders Harland & Wolff Limited, Belfast, Northern Ireland, 1955.
Machinery Steam turbines geared to twin screw; service speed 20 knots.
Capacity 1,100 tourist-class passengers.
Notes The first major liner with engines aft.

1954, 17 Aug Launched by Her Majesty Queen Elizabeth.
1955, 29 Mar Departed from Southampton on first around-the-world cruise, thereafter alternating eastabout and westabout.
1961 Commenced calls at Port Everglades, Florida.
1965 Given new funnel colours.
1971 Mar Withdrawn from service and laid-up.
1972, 26 Apr Moved to the River Fal for further lay-up and offered for sale.
1973 Mar Sold to Compania de Vapores Cerula (Ulysses Line Limited), Greek flag, for £500,000; renamed *Calypso*.
1973, 18 Mar Arrived at Piraeus and commenced major refit.
1975, 20 June Maiden cruise from Tilbury (London) to Scandinavia.
1979 Dec Operated jointly by Paquet and Ulysses Lines for winter cruising from Miami to the Caribbean and summers from Vancouver to Alaska.
1980 Sept Transferred to Western Cruise Lines, Panamanian flag; renamed *Azure Seas*; purchase price $23 million.
1980 Nov Commenced 3- and 4-day cruises from Los Angeles to Mexico.

Despite her rather small size, *Castel Felice* could accommodate 1,405 passengers in a single class (*Alex Duncan*)

Sitmar Line

CASTEL FELICE

Service 1954-8 and 1965: Bremerhaven-Le Havre-Southampton to New York or Quebec City during the summer months only.
Particulars 12,478 tons gross; 493x64x25ft.
Builders Alexander Stephen & Sons Limited, Glasgow, Scotland, 1930.
Machinery Steam turbines geared to twin screw; service speed 17 knots.
Capacity 1,405 tourist-class passengers.

1930, 27 Aug Launched as *Kenya* for British India Steam Navigation Company Limited.
1930 Dec Entered Bombay-Durban service; 9,890 tons gross.
1940-6 Government trooping.
1941 Renamed *Keren*.
1946 Apr Sold to British Ministry of Transport by British India; laid-up.
1949 Renamed *Kenya* and sold to Alva Steamship Company (Sitmar), Panamanian flag.
1950 Renamed *Fairstone*, then reverted to *Kenya* and *Keren*; given Italian registry.
1951-2 Rebuilt at Antwerp and then taken to Genoa for completion: 12,150 tons gross; 1,405 passengers; renamed *Castel Felice*.
1952 Oct Commenced immigrant sailings to Australia and then to South America.
1954 Transatlantic sailings from Bremerhaven to New York and Quebec City.
1955 Refit at Genoa: tonnage relisted as 12,478.
1958 Further transatlantic sailings between Bremerhaven and New York; otherwise Australian sailings.
1965 June Transatlantic sailings to New York for four months; proved uneconomical. Further Australian service.
1969 Mar Transferred from Sitmar Line, Italian flag, to Passenger Line Service Incorporated, Panamanian flag; tonnage relisted as 10,952; retained Sitmar colours and continued in Australian service.
1970, 21 Oct Arrived at Kaohsiung for scrapping.

The former auxiliary aircraft carrier *Fairsea* as she appeared following her 1957-8 refit for passenger service (*Author's Collection*)

FAIRSEA

Service 1953 and 1957: Bremerhaven-Quebec City and Bremerhaven-New York; otherwise Australian immigrant service.
Particulars 11,883 tons gross; 492x69x27ft.
Builders Sun Shipbuilding & Drydock Company, Chester, Pennsylvania, 1941.
Machinery Doxford-type diesels geared to single screw; service speed 16 knots.
Capacity 40 first-class and 1,400 tourist-class passengers.
Notes Former auxiliary aircraft carrier.

1941, 1 Mar Launched as *Rio de la Plata*; combination liner for Moore McCormack Lines, US flag.
1941 Oct Construction handed over to United States Navy; redesigned as auxiliary aircraft carrier *Charger*.
1942 Mar Completed; transferred to British Royal Navy.
1946 Mar Decommissioned and laid-up.
1949 Sold to Alvion Steamship Corporation, Panamanian flag. Rebuilt as a passenger ship; renamed *Fairsea*; tonnage listed as 11,883; capacity 1,440 passengers. Operated by Sitmar Line.
1950 Entered Bremerhaven-Australia immigrant service.
1953, 30 Apr Commenced six sailings Bremerhaven-Quebec City, then back to Australian run.
1957 Several more Atlantic sailings: Bremerhaven-Greenock-Quebec City and Bremerhaven-New York.
1957-8 Rebuilt and modernized at Trieste: tonnage relisted as 13,432; accommodation restyled as 1,460 tourist class; Italian flag.
1958-69 Northern Europe-Australia service; outward via Suez, homeward via Panama.
1969, 29 Jan Serious engine-room fire while 900 miles west of Panama; towed to Balboa by American freighter *Louise Lykes*; laid-up.
1969, 6 Aug Arrived under tow at La Spezia, Italy, for scrapping.

Soviet Ministry of Shipping

ROSSIA

Service 1946-8: Leningrad-New York or Odessa-Mediterranean ports-New York.
Particulars 17,870 tons gross; 584x74x25ft.
Builders Deutsche Werft A/G, Hamburg, Germany, 1938.
Machinery MAN-type diesel-electric engines geared to twin screw; service speed 16 knots.
Capacity Post-war information lacking; pre-war figures listed as 185 first-class and 164 tourist-class passengers.

†1938, 15 June Launched as the *Patria*.
1938, 8 July Severely listed in drydock but recovered with only slight damage.
1938, 12 July Maiden Hamburg-Baltic Sea cruise.
1938, 27 Aug Maiden sailing Hamburg-West Coast of South America via Caribbean and Panama.
1939 Oct Became accommodation ship and floating power station at Stettin.
1942 Moved to Flensburg; continued as accommodation ship.
1945 May Seized by the British invasion forces and used briefly as the seat of the German government.
1945, 1 July Transferred to Great Britain. Refitted at Belfast as a troopship: renamed *Empire Welland*; tonnage increased from 16,595 to 17,870; managed by Furness Withy & Company.
1946 Feb Allocated to the Soviet Government; transferred at Liverpool and renamed *Rossia*.
1946 May First sailing Leningrad-New York.
1947 Feb-1948 Feb Odessa-Mediterranean ports-New York service.
1948 Permanently assigned to local Black Sea service; after 1960, occasional sailings to Havana.

Special Note Several other Soviet liners made a brief number of sailings to the United States in the years 1946-8. Exact information is most difficult to obtain.

Hamburg-America Line's *Patria* as she appeared during her maiden voyage in July 1938 (*World Ship Society Collection*)

As the Soviet Union's *Rossia*, the former kingposts — among other items — have been removed (*Alex Duncan*)

Habana as she appeared after her 1947 refit that included the installation of 112 passenger berths (*Alex Duncan*)

Spanish Line

HABANA

Service Spanish ports-Havana-New York.
Particulars 10,069 tons gross; 500x61x28ft.
Builders Società Española de Construccion Naval, Bilbao, Spain, 1923.
Machinery Steam turbines geared to twin screw; service speed 16 knots.
Capacity 112 first-class passengers.

1920, 14 Sept Launched as *Alfonso XIII* for Spanish Line.
1920, 26 Oct Seriously damaged in shipyard fire.
1923, 19 Sept Maiden voyage Spain-Havana-Vera Cruz; 1,100 passengers in three classes.
1927 Jan Began sailings to New York.
1931 Renamed *Habana*.
1936-9 Laid-up at Bordeaux for safety owing to Spanish Civil War.
1939 Continued sailings to New York and American Gulf Coast.
1943 Seriously damaged by fire at Bilbao; rebuilt as a 12-passenger cargo ship.
1946-7 Thoroughly rebuilt at Brooklyn: fitted with 112 first-class berths; tonnage listed as 10,069. Spain-Havana-New York service.
1953 Cargo sailings only; tonnage reduced to 8,279.
1960 July Laid-up at Ferrol, Spain.
1963-4 Converted to fish factory ship; sold to Pescanova S/A, Spanish flag; tonnage relisted as 10,413; renamed *Galicia*.

Marques de Comillas originally had two funnels and two masts (*Alex Duncan*)

MARQUES DE COMILLAS

Service Spanish ports-Havana-New York.
Particulars 9,922 tons gross; 467x56x25ft.
Builders Società Española de Construccion Naval, Ferrol, Spain, 1928.
Machinery Steam turbines geared to twin screw; service speed 16 knots.
Capacity 241 first class and 221 tourist class.

1927 Mar Damaged during launching.
1928 Nov Maiden voyage Cadiz-New York; 150 first class and 400 tourist class.
1936-9 Laid-up for safety during Spanish Civil War.
1939 Oct Resumed Spain-Havana-New York sailings.
1953 Transferred to Spain-West Indies-Mexico service.
1961 Jan Commenced major refit: accommodation restyled as 134 special tourist and 796 tourist class.
1961 Nov Damaged by fire at shipyard at Ferrol, Spain.
1962 Mar Arrived at Bilbao for scrapping.

At completion *Covadonga* made a Coronation cruise to London from Spain (*Spanish Line*)

COVADONGA

Service Bilbao-Santander-Gijon-Vigo-Lisbon-New York-Havana or San Juan-Vera Cruz-New York-Corunna-Santander-Bilbao.
Particulars 10,226 tons gross; 487x62x26ft.
Builders Compania Euskalduna, Bilbao, Spain, 1953.
Machinery Sulzer-type diesel geared to single screw; service speed 16.5 knots.
Capacity 105 first class and 248 tourist class.

1952 Launched as *Monasterio de la Rabida*; cargo ship for Compania Empresa Nacional Elcano, Spanish flag. Sold to Spanish Line shortly after launching and redesigned as a passenger-cargo ship.
1953 May Coronation cruise Spain-London.
1953, 27 Aug Maiden voyage Bilbao-Santander-Gijon-Vigo-Lisbon-New York-Havana-Vera Cruz.
1973, 19 Jan Laid-up at Bilbao.
1973, 4 Apr Arrived at Castellon for scrapping.

Just before her sale to Spanish breakers it was rumoured that *Guadalupe* would become an Indian Ocean pilgrim ship (*Spanish Line*)

GUADALUPE

Service Bilbao-Santander-Gijon-Vigo-Lisbon-New York-Havana or San Juan-Vera Cruz-New York-Corunna-Santander-Bilbao.
Particulars 10,226 tons gross; 487x62x26ft.
Builders Società Española de Construccion Naval, Bilbao, Spain, 1953.
Machinery Sulzer-type diesel geared to single screw; service speed 16.5 knots.
Capacity 105 first class and 244 tourist class.

1952 Launched as *Monasterio de Guadalupe*; cargo ship for Compania Empresa Nacional Elcano, Spanish flag. Sold to Spanish Line shortly after launching and redesigned as a passenger-cargo ship.
1953, 21 Mar Maiden voyage Spanish ports-New York-Havana-Vera Cruz.
1973, 10 Apr Arrived at Castellon for scrapping.

The combination passenger-cargo ship *Bothinj* and her two sisters were transferred to Rijeka-West Africa service before scrapping (*Michael D. J. Lennon*)

Splosna Plovba

BOTHINJ

Service Rijeka-New York, occasionally via other ports.
Particulars 7,746 tons gross; 448x57x26ft.
Builders Cockerill S/A Shipyard, Hoboken, Belgium, 1941-6.
Machinery B&W-type diesel geared to single screw; service speed 14 knots.
Capacity 14 first class and 56 tourist class.

1941 Launched by Nazi Invasion Forces.
1944 Scuttled in the River Scheldt by the retreating armies.
1946 Completed as *Gouverneur Galopin* for Compagnie Maritime Belge, Belgian flag; Antwerp-Congo service.
1959 Sold to Splosna Plovba, Yugoslavian flag; renamed *Bothinj*; Rijeka-New York service.
1972, 12 Jan Left Rijeka for Split for scrapping by Brodospas.

BOVEC

Service Rijeka-New York, occasionally via other ports.
Particulars 7,766 tons gross; 448x57x26ft.
Builders Cockerill S/A Shipyard, Hoboken, Belgium, 1941-5.
Machinery B&W-type diesel geared to single screw; service speed 14 knots.
Capacity 14 first class and 56 tourist class.

1941 Launched by Nazi Invasion Forces.
1944 Scuttled in River Scheldt by the retreating armies.
1946 Completed as *Armand Grisar* for Compagnie Maritime Belge, Belgian flag; Antwerp-Congo service.
1959 Sold to Splosna Plovba, Yugoslavian flag; renamed *Bovec*; Rijeka-New York service.
1970 Dec Sold to Chinese shipbreakers and scrapped at Whampoa.

BLED

Service Rijeka-New York, occasionally via other ports.
Particulars 7,761 tons gross; 448x57x26ft.
Builders Cockerill S/A Shipyard, Hoboken, Belgium, 1942-5.
Machinery B&W-type diesel geared to single screw; service speed 14 knots.
Capacity 60 tourist class.

1942 Launched as German freighter *Kanomier*.
1945 Found in the Baltic; returned to Belgium.
1946 Rebuilt for Compagnie Maritime Belge, Belgian flag; renamed *Alex van Opstal*; Antwerp-Congo service.
1959 Sold to Splosna Plovba, Yugoslavian flag; renamed *Bled*; Rijeka-New York service.
1970 Scrapped at La Spezia, Italy.

The hull of *Drottningholm* was repainted in white in 1932. In addition to regular transatlantic service she made occasional cruises (*Michael Cassar*)

Swedish American Line

DROTTNINGHOLM

Service Gothenburg-Copenhagen-New York; occasional westbound calls at Halifax.
Particulars 10,249 tons gross; 538x60ft.
Builders Alexander Stephen & Sons Limited, Glasgow, Scotland, 1905.
Machinery Steam turbines geared to triple screw; service speed 18 knots.
Capacity 532 first class and 854 tourist class.
Notes First Atlantic liner to be fitted with direct-action turbines.

1904, 22 Dec Launched.
1905 Apr Maiden voyage as *Virginian* for Allan Line, British flag. Liverpool-Saint John, NB, service; to Montreal during the summers.
1914-20 Auxiliary cruiser and troopship.
1915 Oct Transferred to Canadian Pacific Steamships, British flag; retained her name.
1920 Feb Sold to Swedish American Line, Swedish flag; renamed *Drottningholm*.
1920 May Maiden voyage Gothenburg-New York. 426 first class, 286 second class and 1,000 third class.
1922 Given new turbines; tonnage listed as 11,182; passenger accommodation restyled as 532 cabin class and 854 third class.
1932 Hull repainted in white.
1940-6 Used as International Red Cross 'exchange ship' for diplomats, refugees, prisoners, etc.
1946 Mar First Swedish American post-war sailing Gothenburg-New York; sold to Home Lines but delivery postponed until 1948.
1948 Transferred to Home Lines, Panamanian flag; renamed *Brasil* (qv).

Gripsholm departing on her maiden voyage from Gothenburg in November 1925 (*Swedish American Line*)

The same liner following her 1949 refit; notice the wider funnels (*Swedish American Line*)

GRIPSHOLM

Service Gothenburg-Copenhagen-New York; sometimes via Halifax (westbound).
Particulars 19,105 tons gross; 590x74x29ft.
Builders Sir W. G. Armstrong-Whitworth & Company, Newcastle, England, 1925.
Machinery B&W-type diesels geared to twin screw; service speed 16.5 knots.
Capacity 210 first class and 710 tourist class.
Notes First transatlantic liner to be driven by diesels.

1924, 26 Nov Launched.
1925, 21 Nov Maiden voyage Gothenburg-New York: 17,993 tons gross; 127 first class, 482 second class and 948 third class. Transatlantic service and worldwide cruising.
1932 Repainted with white hull.
1937 Major refit: tonnage relisted as 18,134.
1940-6 Used as International Red Cross 'exchange ship' for diplomats, refugees, prisoners, etc.
1946 Mar Resumed Gothenburg-New York sailings.
1949-50 Major refit at Kiel: new funnels fitted; accommodation modernized and restyled as 210 first class and 910 tourist class; given new bow and lengthened from 573 to 590ft; tonnage listed as 19,105.
1953, 29 Dec Final sailing Gothenburg-New York.
1954, 1 Feb Began sailing for Bremen-America Line (a partnership firm of Swedish American and North German Lloyd); retained name. Bremerhaven-New York service.
1955 Jan Purchased outright by North German Lloyd, West German flag; renamed *Berlin* (qv).

STOCKHOLM

Service Gothenburg-Copenhagen-New York; sometimes via Halifax (westbound). Cruising.
Particulars 11,700 tons gross; 525x69x24ft.
Builders A/B Gotaverken Shipyard, Gothenburg, Sweden, 1948.
Machinery Gotaverken-type diesels geared to twin screw; service speed 19 knots.
Capacity 113 first class and 282 tourist class.
Notes Became the world's first trade-union holiday ship in 1960.

1946, 9 Sept Launched; first transatlantic liner to be launched after the War and the largest passenger ship ever built in Sweden.
1948, 21 Feb Maiden voyage Gothenburg-New York.
1952 Major refit: accommodation restyled as 86 first class and 584 tourist class; tonnage relisted as 12,644.
1955 First-class accommodation reduced to 24 berths.
1956 Feb Rumoured to be transferring to newly-formed Denmark-America Line for Copenhagen-New York service; never materialized.
1956, 25 July Rammed and sank the Italian liner *Andrea Doria* in fog off Nantucket; 52 casualties.
1956, 8 Dec Returned to service after thorough repairs including new bow fitted by Bethlehem Steel Company, Brooklyn.
1960, 3 Jan Delivered to Deutsche Seereederi, East German flag. Renamed *Volkerfreundschaft*; 568 one-class passengers; tonnage listed as 12,387. World's first trade-union holiday ship: year-round cruising from Rostock.
1960 Aug Grounded at Sandhamn.
1972 Remeasured at 12,068 tons gross.

KUNGSHOLM

Service Gothenburg-Copenhagen-New York; occasionally including Bremerhaven and Halifax (westbound). Considerable cruising.
Particulars 21,141 tons gross; 600x77x26ft.
Builders De Schelde Shipyard, Flushing, Holland, 1953.
Machinery B&W-type diesels geared to twin screw; service speed 19 knots.
Capacity 176 first class and 626 tourist class.

1952, 18 Apr Launched by Her Royal Highness Princess Sybilla of Sweden.
1953, 24 Nov Left Gothenburg on maiden voyage to New York.
1961 Nov Refit.
1965, 16 Oct Delivered to North German Lloyd, West German flag; renamed *Europa* (qv).

GRIPSHOLM

Service Gothenburg-Copenhagen-New York; considerable cruising.
Particulars 23,191 tons gross; 631x82x27ft.
Builders Ansaldo Shipyard, Genoa, Italy, 1957.
Machinery Gotaverken-type diesels geared to twin screw; service speed 19 knots.
Capacity 214 first class and 628 tourist class.

1955, 10 May Laid down.
1956, 8 Apr Launched by Her Royal Highness Princess Margaretha of Sweden.
1957, 14 May Left Gothenburg on maiden voyage to New York.
1974 Oct Plans abandoned to transfer ship to Panamanian flag.
1975, 26 Aug Withdrawn and laid-up; offered for sale.
1975, 19 Dec Reported sold to Karageorgis Cruises (Nautilus Armadora S/A), Greek flag; renamed *Navarino*. Refitted for Mediterranean and South African cruising.

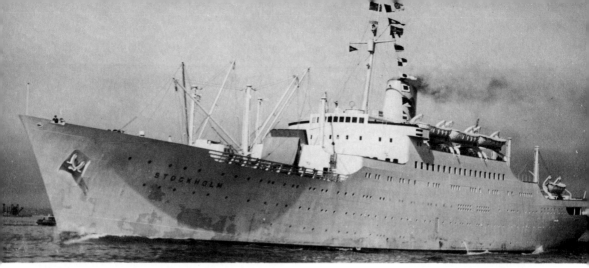

Stockholm as originally built in 1948 (*Roger Scozzafava*)

Kungsholm was the first major Atlantic liner to have all-outside passenger cabins (*Swedish American Line*)

The beautiful *Gripsholm* during a cruise (*Michael D. J. Lennon*)

The swimming pool aboard *Kungsholm* was placed between the funnels, the forward of which was a dummy (*Swedish American Line*)

KUNGSHOLM

Service Gothenburg-Copenhagen-New York; mostly cruising.
Particulars 26,678 tons gross; 660x86x26ft.
Builders John Brown & Company Limited, Clydebank, Scotland, 1966.
Machinery Gotaverken-type diesels geared to twin screw; service speed 21 knots.
Capacity 108 first class and 642 tourist class; 450 one-class for cruising.

1965, 14 Apr Launched.
1966, 11 Mar Transferred to drydock at Belfast; completion delayed by three months; total cost $22 million.
1966, 2 May Arrived in New York on maiden voyage from Gothenburg.
1974 Oct Plans shelved for transfer to Panamanian registry.
1975 Dec Withdrawn and laid-up, thus ending Swedish American passenger service. Sold to Oivind Lorentzen (Flagship Cruises), Liberian flag; retained name; cruising only.
1978, 14 Jan Refloating began in Fort de France Bay after going aground. Completed on 19 January.
1978 Sept Sold and delivered to Sea Leasing Corporation, British flag; operated by P&O Cruises Limited; renamed *Sea Princess*. Major refit at Bremerhaven: forward funnel removed.
1979, 20 Jan Departed for Hong Kong; based at Sydney for Pacific cruising.

Tarsus was destroyed after colliding with a blazing tanker in the Bosphorus (*Alex Duncan*)

Turkish Maritime Lines

TARSUS

Service Periodic Istanbul-New York sailings; otherwise local Mediterranean service and cruising.
Particulars 9,451 tons gross; 475x62x27ft.
Builders New York Shipbuilding Company, Camden, New Jersey, 1931.
Machinery Steam turbines geared to single screw; service speed 16 knots.
Capacity 189 first class, 66 second class and 210 third class.
Notes 1946-60: flagship of the Turkish Merchant Marine.

1930 Launched as *Exochorda* for American Export Lines, US flag.
1931 Maiden voyage New York-Mediterranean ports: 125 first-class passengers; 9,360 tons gross.
1940 Oct Acquired by United States Navy; renamed USS *Harry Lee*.
1941-6 Transport work.
1946 Declared surplus. Sold to Turkish Maritime Lines, Turkish flag; renamed *Tarsus*. Major refit: tonnage relisted as 9,451; accommodation restyled as 189 first class, 66 second class and 210 third class.
1960 June Chartered to Fiesta Cruise Lines for New York-Bermuda service.
1960 Dec Destroyed by fire in the Bosphorus after being rammed by blazing ship following collision of tankers *Peter Zoranic* and *World Harmony*.

Washington as she appeared following extensive duty as a wartime troopship; notice the military-type radar mast just forward of the first funnel (*Alex Duncan*)

United States Lines

WASHINGTON

Service Post-war 'austerity service' New York-Cobh-Le Havre-Southampton; sometimes to Bremerhaven.
Particulars 29,627 tons gross; 705x86ft.
Builders New York Shipbuilding Company, Camden, New Jersey, 1933.
Machinery Steam turbines geared to twin screw; service speed 20 knots.
Capacity Post-war: 1,106 berths, single 'austerity class'.

1932, 20 Aug Launched.
1933, 10 May Maiden voyage New York-Southampton-Le Havre-Hamburg: 24,289 tons gross; 580 cabin class, 400 tourist class and 150 third class.
1940-1 Cruising from New York owing to outbreak of War in Europe.
1941 June Commenced major refit for US Navy: converted to troopship; renamed *Mount Vernon*.
1942 Sept Sold to the US Government.
1945 Reverted to name *Washington*.
1946 Jan Operated by US Maritime Commission.
1948 Feb Resumed New York-Southampton-Bremerhaven 'austerity service'; chartered to United States Lines.
1951, 12 Oct Withdrawn from North Atlantic service.
1952 Laid-up in Hudson River Reserve Fleet at Jones Point, New York.
1964, 30 June Sold by US Department of Commerce to Union Minerals & Alloys Corporation for $238,126.
1965, 28 June Arrived in tow at Kearny, New Jersey, for scrapping.

MARINE PERCH

Service New York-Southampton-Le Havre; sometimes to other European ports; 'austerity service'.
Particulars 12,410 tons gross; 523x74x24ft.
Builders Kaiser Company Incorporated, Richmond, California, 1945.
Machinery Steam turbines geared to single screw; service speed 17 knots.
Capacity 550 single class for 'austerity service'; otherwise up to 3,000 troops.

1945, 25 June Launched.
1945 Oct Completed for transport service.
1946 Commenced charter to United States Lines for 'austerity service'.
1948 Returned to the Maritime Commission and laid-up.
1965 Sold to Rio Grande Transport Incorporated. Rebuilt as a bulk carrier: 11,034 tons gross; renamed *Yellowstone*.
1978, 14 June Sunk off Gibraltar following collision with Algerian flag *Liban Batouata*.

MARINE MARLIN

Service New York-Southampton-Le Havre; sometimes to Bremerhaven and other European ports.
Particulars 12,420 tons gross; 523x74x24ft.
Builders Kaiser Company Incorporated, Vancouver, Washington, 1945.
Machinery Steam turbines geared to single screw; service speed 17 knots.
Capacity 550 single class for 'austerity service'; otherwise up to 3,000 troops.

1945, 28 July Launched.
1945 Dec Entered transport service.
1946 Sept Commenced charter to United States Lines for 'austerity service'.
1949 Returned to Maritime Commission and laid-up.
1965 Sold to Central Gulf Steamship Company and rebuilt as a freighter: renamed *Green Bay*; 11,021 tons gross.
1971, 17 Aug Sank at Qui Nhon, South Vietnam, after underwater explosion.
1971, 31 Aug Raised; beyond economic repair.
1971, 1 Oct Arrived in tow at Hong Kong for scrapping.

MARINE FALCON

Service New York-Southampton-Le Havre; sometimes to Bremerhaven and other European ports; 'austerity service'.
Particulars 12,420 tons gross; 523x74x24ft.
Builders Kaiser Company Incorporated, Vancouver, Washington, 1945.
Machinery Steam turbines geared to single screw; service speed 17 knots.
Capacity 550 single class for 'austerity service'; otherwise up to 3,000 troops.

1945, 27 Apr Launched.
1945 Sept Completed and began transport service.
1947 Apr Commenced charter to United States Lines for 'austerity service'.
1948 Returned to Maritime Commission and laid-up.
1966 Sold to Sea-Land Service and rebuilt as the containership *Trenton*: tonnage relisted as 17,189; lengthened to 684ft.
1975 Transferred to Navieras de Puerto Rico, US flag; renamed *Borinquen*.

Special Note All 'Marine' class troopships did spells of service between 1946-9 for American President, American Export and Moore McCormack lines to both Northern Europe and the Mediterranean.

MARINE FLASHER

Service New York-Southampton-Le Havre; sometimes to Bremerhaven and other European ports; 'austerity service'.
Particulars 12,558 tons gross; 523x74x24ft.
Builders Kaiser Company Incorporated, Vancouver, Washington, 1945.
Machinery Steam turbines geared to single screw; service speed 17 knots.
Capacity 550 single class for 'austerity service'; otherwise up to 3,000 troops.

1945, 16 May Launched.
1945 Sept Entered transport service.
1946 May Chartered to United States Lines for transatlantic 'austerity service'.
1949 Sept Returned to Maritime Commission and laid-up.
1966 Sold to Sea-Land Service (Litton Industries Leasing Corporation). Rebuilt as a containership at Ingalls Shipyard, Pascagoula, Mississippi; 17,814 tons gross; 684ft long; renamed *Long Beach*.

Marine Flasher photographed at the Kaiser Company Yard at Vancouver, Washington, on 21 August 1945 (*Frank O. Braynard Collection*)

The former *Marine Flasher*, rebuilt in 1966 as a containership and shown passing through the Panama Canal as the *Long Beach* (*Sea-Land Industries*)

Ernie Pyle at dock in 1949 (*Ernest Arroyo Collection*)

ERNIE PYLE

Service New York-Southampton-Le Havre; sometimes to Bremerhaven and other European ports; 'austerity service'.
Particulars 12,420 tons gross; 523x74x24ft.
Builders Kaiser Company Incorporated, Vancouver, Washington, 1945.
Machinery Steam turbines geared to single screw; service speed 17 knots.
Capacity 550 single class for 'austerity service'; otherwise up to 3,000 troops.

1945, 25 June Launched.
1945 Nov Commenced transport service.
1946 June Began United States Lines charter.
1949 Returned to Maritime Commission and laid-up.
1965 Sold to Central Gulf Steamship Company and rebuilt as a freighter: renamed *Green Lake*; tonnage listed as 11,021.
1980 No longer in service.

Enlarged to 684ft the former *Marine Jumper* is seen as the containership *Panama* (*Sea-Land Industries*)

MARINE JUMPER

Service New York-Southampton-Le Havre; sometimes to Bremerhaven and other European ports; 'austerity service'.
Particulars 12,420 tons gross; 523x74x24ft.
Builders Kaiser Company Incorporated, Vancouver, Washington, 1945.
Machinery Steam turbines geared to single screw; service speed 17 knots.
Capacity 550 single class for 'austerity service'; otherwise up to 3,000 troops.

1945, 30 May Launched.
1945 Oct Entered transport service.
1947 Chartered to United States Lines for 'austerity service'.
1949 Returned to Maritime Commission and laid-up.
1966 Sold to Sea-Land Service and rebuilt as the containership *Panama*: tonnage revised to 17,184; lengthened to 684ft.

Marine Shark in New York Harbour in January 1947 (*Frank O. Braynard Collection*)

Unlike some of her other former sisterships, the *Marine Shark* was not lengthened but merely rebuilt as the container carrier *Charleston* (*Sea-Land Industries*)

MARINE SHARK

Service New York-Southampton-Le Havre; sometimes to Bremerhaven and other European ports.
Particulars 12,558 tons gross; 523x74x24ft.
Builders Kaiser Company Incorporated, Vancouver, Washington, 1945.
Machinery Steam turbines geared to single screw; service speed 17 knots.
Capacity 550 single class for 'austerity service'; otherwise up to 3,000 troops.

1945, 4 Apr Launched.
1945 Sept Began transport service.
1948 May Commenced charter to United States Lines.
1949 Returned to Maritime Commission and laid-up.
1967 Sold to Sea-Land Service and rebuilt as a containership: renamed *Charleston*; tonnage relisted as 11,389.
1980, 4 Apr Heavy damage to bottom after running aground off Block Island, USA; later repaired.

MARINE TIGER

Service New York-Southampton-Le Havre; sometimes to Bremerhaven and other European ports.
Particulars 12,558 tons gross; 523x74x24ft.
Builders Kaiser Company Incorporated, Vancouver, Washington, 1945.
Machinery Steam turbines geared to single screw; service speed 17 knots.
Capacity 550 single class for 'austerity service'; otherwise up to 3,000 troops.

1945, 23 Mar Launched.
1945 July Entered transport service.
1947 June Commenced charter to United States Lines.
1949 Sept Returned to Maritime Commission and laid-up.
1966 Sold to Sea-Land Service and rebuilt as a containership: renamed *Oakland*; tonnage relisted as 17,184; lengthened to 684ft.

AMERICA

Service New York-Cobh-Le Havre-Southampton-Bremerhaven.
Particulars 33,532 tons gross; 723x93x29ft.
Builders Newport News Shipbuilding & Drydock Company, Newport News, Virginia, 1940.
Machinery Steam turbines geared to twin screw; service speed 22 knots.
Capacity 516 first class, 371 cabin class and 159 tourist class.
Notes Flagship of the US Merchant Marine 1940-52.

1937, 21 Oct Ordered.
1938, 22 Aug Keel laid.
1939, 31 Aug Launched by Mrs Franklin D. Roosevelt.
1940 July Completed; tonnage 26,424.
1940 Aug Began cruising from New York owing to war in Europe.
1941-6 Trooping for the US Navy.
1942 Renamed USS *West Point*.
1946, 22 July Decomissioned; reverted to name *America*; major refit.
1946, 14 Nov First post-war commercial sailing.
1949 Nov Tonnage relisted as 33,532.
1960 Dec Refit: accommodation restyled as 516 first class and 530 tourist class.
1963 Sept Six-month lay-up at Todd Shipyards, Hoboken, as a result of labour dispute; returned to service February 1964.
1964, 28 Aug Sold to Okeania S/A (Chandris Group), Greek flag, for £1.5 million.
1964 Nov Delivered to new owners at Newport News, Virginia; renamed *Australis* (qv).

In peacetime colours, *America* is docked at Bremerhaven in the early 1950s with *Washington* further beyond (*United States Lines*)

USS *West Point* arriving at New York with over 5,000 troops onboard during the summer of 1945. The troopship *Monticello* (ex-*Conte Grande*) is docked at the left (*United States Navy*)

UNITED STATES

Service New York-Le Havre-Southampton-Bremerhaven; off-season cruising.
Particulars 53,329 tons gross; 990x101x28ft.
Builders Newport News Shipbuilding & Drydock Company, Newport News, Virginia, 1952.
Machinery Steam turbines geared to quadruple screw; service speed 30 knots.
Capacity 871 first class, 508 cabin class and 551 tourist class.
Notes World's fastest passenger liner; flagship of the American Merchant Marine.

1950, 8 Feb Laid down.
1951, 23 June Floated in drydock (not launched).
1952 June Highly successful trials; cost $77 million.
1952, 3 July Maiden sailing: captured Blue Riband with a crossing to England that averaged 35.39 knots.
1969, 23 Jan Began longest sailing of her career: 39 days to South America and Africa, a total of 19,000 miles.
1969, 1 May First call at Boston as part of an Atlantic crossing.
1969, 8 Nov Arrived at Newport News Shipyard; laid-up indefinitely at Norfolk.
1973 Apr Sold to the US Federal Government for $4.6 million; continued in lay-up.
1978 Nov Reportedly sold to United States Cruises Incorporated for $5 million.
1979 Sept Proposed that, as a cruiseship, the *United States* should sail between California and Hawaii as well as occasional long-distance cruises; planned for 1,700 one-class passengers. Reactivation project sluggish.
1980 May Drydocked at Norfolk for the first time in nearly 11 years; returned to lay-up status.
1980 Aug Reported to be under consideration by the US Navy for conversion into a hospital ship for operations in the Middle East.

The world's fastest liner being eased into drydock at Newport News, Virginia. Note the nuclear aircraft carrier *Enterprise* just beyond the liner's forward funnel (*United States Lines*)

United States docking at New York during her maiden arrival in July 1952 (*United States Lines*)

Jerusalem was the first sizeable passenger ship in the Israeli fleet (*Zim Lines*)

Zim Lines

JERUSALEM

Service Haifa-Piraeus-Malta-Ceuta-Halifax-New York-Ceuta-Piraeus-Haifa; also Haifa-Marseilles service.
Particulars 11,015 tons gross; 530x61ft.
Builders Cammell Laird & Company Limited, Birkenhead, England, 1913.
Machinery Steam turbines geared to twin screw; service speed 15 knots.
Capacity 32 first class and 741 tourist class.
Notes First Atlantic liner in the Israeli Merchant Marine.

1913-46 Sailed as *Bergensfjord* for Norwegian America Line.
1946-53 Sailed as *Argentina* for Home Lines (qv).
1953 Feb Purchased by Zim Lines, Israeli flag; renamed *Jerusalem*.
1953, 29 Apr Departed from Haifa on first sailing to New York.
1955 Permanently assigned to Haifa-Marseilles service.
1957 Renamed *Aliya*.
1958 Laid-up.
1959, 13 Aug Arrived at La Spezia for scrapping.

Israel was the first brand-new passenger ship in the Israeli Merchant Marine as well as for Zim Lines itself. She and her sistership were built in West Germany as part of a Wartime Reparations Pact (*Zim Lines*)

As *Angra do Heroismo*, she was painted with a black hull (*Alex Duncan*)

ISRAEL

Service Haifa-Piraeus-Naples-Palma-Gibraltar-Halifax-New York-Gibraltar-Palma-Naples-Piraeus-Haifa; ports varied and call at Halifax sometimes eliminated.
Particulars 9,853 tons gross; 501x65x27ft.
Builders Deutsche Werft A/G, Hamburg, West Germany, 1955.
Machinery Steam turbines geared to single screw; service speed 18 knots.
Capacity 24 first class, 232 tourist class and 56 interchangeable.
Notes The first liner built for Israeli interests.

1955, 4 Mar Launched.
1955, 24 Sept Maiden voyage Hamburg-Southampton-Haifa.
1955, 13 Oct Departed from Haifa on maiden voyage to New York.
1959, 29 Oct Rammed by freighter *American Press* in New York harbour; one crewman killed; towed to Brooklyn shipyard.
1966, 25 Mar Withdrawn from Zim passenger service.
1966 Sold to Empresa Insulana, Portuguese flag; renamed *Angra Do Heroismo*. Lisbon-Madeira-Azores service.
1974 Scrapped at Castellon, Spain.

ZION

Service Haifa-Piraeus-Naples-Palma-Gibraltar-Halifax-New York-Gibraltar-Palma-Naples-Piraeus-Haifa; ports varied and call at Halifax sometimes eliminated.
Particulars 9,855 tons gross; 501x65x27ft.
Builders Deutsche Werft A/G, Hamburg, West Germany, 1956.
Machinery Steam turbines geared to single screw; service speed 18 knots.
Capacity 24 first class, 232 tourist class and 56 interchangeable.

1955, 19 July Launched.
1956, 19 Feb Maiden voyage Hamburg-Le Havre-Southampton-Messina-Haifa.
1956, 9 Mar Departed from Haifa on maiden voyage to New York.
1966, 14 Apr Withdrawn from Zim passenger service.
1966 Sold to Soc. Geral de Commercio Ind. e Transportes, Portuguese flag; sale price $2.3 million. Renamed *Amelia de Mello*; Lisbon-Canaries-Azores service; tonnage relisted as 10,195.
1971 Aug Laid-up at Lisbon; offered for sale.
1972 Sold to Ulysses Line (Compania de Vapores Realma S/A), Greek flag; renamed *Ithaca*.
1972, 9 May Arrived at Bilbao for rebuilding as a cruiseship: fitted with 780 first-class berths; tonnage relisted as 8,977. Mediterranean cruising.
1978 Transferred to Panamanian flag; renamed *Dolphin IV*.
1979 Jan Commenced Miami-Bahamas service.

JERUSALEM

Service Periodic transatlantic crossings: Haifa-Limassol-Piraeus-Naples-Gibraltar-New York; otherwise Haifa-Marseilles service; winter cruising from New York to the Caribbean.
Particulars 9,920 tons gross; 487x65x21ft.
Builders Deutsche Werft A/G, Hamburg, West Germany, 1957.
Machinery Steam turbines geared to twin screw; service speed 18 knots.
Capacity 102 first class and 471 tourist class.

1958 Commissioned by Zim Lines for Haifa-Marseilles service and occasional transatlantic sailings; winter cruising.
1964 Converted for more extensive cruise work by Ocean Shipyard, Haifa.
1966 Commenced three-year charter to Peninsular & Occidental Steamship Company, Miami, for Miami-Bahamas service; renamed *Miami*.
1968 Charter cancelled. Sold to Eastern Steamship Lines (Miami Steamship Company), Liberia; renamed *New Bahama Star*. Given major refit costing $5 million; original steam whistle transferred from predeccessor *Bahama Star* (ex-*Arosa Star* qv).
1969, 10 Mar Maiden voyage Miami-Nassau.
1969, 31 Oct Grounded off Miami; later refloated.
1972 Renamed *Bahama Star*; transferred to Bahamas Shipping Corporation, Liberian flag. Continued in Miami-Nassau service for Eastern Steamship Lines.
1974, 27 Oct Boiler damage.
1975 Sold to Venzolana de Cruceros del Caribe, Venezuelan flag; renamed *Bonaire Star*. Laid-up at Mobile; never sailed.
1979 Apr Sold for scrap to Southern Metals Company for $322,000.
1979, 8 May Left Mobile under tow for New Orleans.
1979 May Resold to West German buyers and then sold again to scrappers at Kaohsiung, Taiwan.
1979, 3 Oct Sank in Pacific while being towed by tug *Jantar*.

Jerusalem was designed for both inter-European and transatlantic services as well as for cruising. Her sistership was named *Theodor Herzl* (*Zim Lines*)

The ex-*Jerusalem* sailed to and from the Port of Miami as *New Bahama Star* (*Eastern Steamship Lines*)

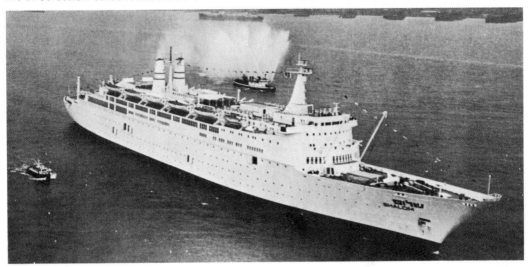

Shalom shown during her maiden arrival at New York in April 1964 (*Zim Lines*)

SHALOM

Service Haifa-Náples-Marseilles-Malaga-New York; occasionally via other Mediterranean ports; considerable cruising.
Particulars 25,320 tons gross; 629x82x26ft.
Builders Chantiers de l'Atlantique, St Nazaire, France, 1964.
Machinery Steam turbines geared to twin screw; service speed 20 knots.
Capacity 72 first class and 1,018 tourist class.
Notes Flagship of Israeli Merchant Marine 1964-7.

1962, 10 Nov Launched by Mrs David Ben-Gurion; original intention was to name ship as *King Solomon* and then as *King David*; cost £7.5 million.
1964, 17 Apr Left Haifa on maiden voyage to New York.
1964, 18 Oct Arrived at Wilton-Fijenoord Shipyard, Schiedam, Holland, for the installation of an additional 76 first-class passenger berths.
1964, 26 Nov Rammed Norwegian tanker *Stolt Dagali* some 28 miles southeast of Ambrose Light, New York; the stern section of the tanker sank; 19 casualties. *Shalom* had $575,000 worth of damage; repaired at Todd Shipyards, Brooklyn.
1967 May Sold to German-Atlantic Line for £5.6 million.
1967 Nov Delivered to German-Atlantic, West German flag; renamed *Hanseatic* (qv).

Appendix

25 Largest Transatlantic Liners from 1945

		Tonnage	Company	Flag
1	*Queen Elizabeth*	83,673	Cunard Line	British
2	*Queen Mary*	81,237	Cunard Line	British
3	*Queen Elizabeth 2*	67,107	Cunard Line	British
4	*France*	66,348	French Line	French
5	*United States*	53,329	US Lines	American
6	*Liberté*	51,839	French Line	French
7	*Raffaello*	45,933	Italian Line	Italian
8	*Michelangelo*	45,911	Italian Line	Italian
9	*Canberra*	45,733	P&O-Orient	British
10	*Aquitania*	45,647	Cunard Line	British
11	*Ile de France*	44,356	French Line	French
12	*Oriana*	41,923	P&O-Orient	British
13	*Rotterdam*	38,645	Holland-America	Dutch
14	*Nieuw Amsterdam*	36,667	Holland-America	Dutch
15	*Mauretania*	35,655	Cunard Line	British
16	*Australis*	34,449	Chandris Lines	Panamanian/Greek
	ex-*America*	(33,532)	US Lines	American
17	*Caronia*	34,172	Cunard Line	British
18	*Leonardo da Vinci*	33,340	Italian Line	Italian
19	*Bremen*	32,336	North German Lloyd	West German
20	*Independence*	30,293	American Export	American
21	*Constitution*	30,293	American Export	American
22	*Hanseatic*	30,029	Hamburg-Atlantic	West German
23	*Iberia*	29,734	P&O-Orient	British
24	*Arcadia*	29,614	P&O-Orient	British
25	*Cristoforo Colombo*	29,191	Italian Line	Italian

25 Longest Transatlantic Liners from 1945

		Length (in feet)	Company	Flag
1	*France*	1,035	French Line	French
2	*Queen Elizabeth*	1,031	Cunard Line	British
3	*Queen Mary*	1,018	Cunard Line	British
4	*United States*	990	US Lines	American
5	*Queen Elizabeth 2*	963	Cunard Line	British
6	*Liberté*	936	French Line	French
7	*Michelangelo*	902	Italian Line	Italian
8	*Raffaello*	902	Italian Line	Italian
9	*Aquitania*	901	Cunard Line	British
10	*Canberra*	818	P&O-Orient	British
11	*Oriana*	804	P&O-Orient	British
12	*Ile de France*	792	French Line	French
13	*Mauretania*	772	Cunard Line	British
14	*Leonardo da Vinci*	761	Italian Line	Italian
15	*Nieuw Amsterdam*	758	Holland-America	Dutch
16	*Rotterdam*	748	Holland-America	Dutch
17	*Australis*	723	Chandris Lines	Panamanian/Greek
	(ex-*America*)	(723)	US Lines	American
18	*Orsova*	723	P&O-Orient	British
19	*Iberia*	721	P&O-Orient	British
20	*Arcadia*	719	P&O-Orient	British
21	*Caronia*	715	Cunard Line	British
22	*Britannic*	712	Cunard Line	British
23	*Georgic*	711	Cunard Line	British
24	*Orcades*	709	P&O-Orient	British
25	*Himalaya*	709	P&O-Orient	British

Index of Passenger Ships